ANTI INFLAMMATORY COOKBOOK

Reinforce Immune Defenses, Reduce Inflammation, Reduce Chronic Pain, and Empower Your Health at Any Age through Easy and Delicious Recipes. 60-Day Meal Plan.

Olivia Davis

Table of Content

What is the Anti-Inflammatory Diet?	3
Biology of Inflammation	3
Triggers of Chronic Inflammation	3
Link Between Inflammation & Chronic Diseases	4
Recognizing Symptoms of Inflammation	5
Lifestyle: Finding Balance for Well-being	6
Benefits of an Anti-Inflammatory Diet	6
Key Principles and Guidelines	7
Foods to Include and Avoid	9

BREAKFAST — 11

1. Turmeric Scrambled Eggs with Spinach — 12
2. Quinoa Breakfast Bowl — 12
3. Avocado Toast with Salmon — 12
4. Chia Seed Pudding with Berries — 12
5. Oatmeal with Walnuts & Blueberries — 13
6. Sweet Potato and Kale Hash — 13
7. Greek Yogurt Parfait — 13
8. Salmon and Spinach Omelette — 13
9. Green Smoothie Bowl — 14
10. Almond Flour Pancakes — 14
11. Coconut and Berry Overnight Oats — 14
12. Veggie Frittata with Turmeric — 15
13. Buckwheat Pancakes — 15
14. Banana Walnut Muffins — 15
15. Spinach and Mushroom Wrap — 16
16. Quinoa Porridge Cinnamon Apples — 16
17. Blueberry and Almond Smoothie — 16
18. Smashed Avocado & Tomato Toast — 16
19. Berry Protein Smoothie — 17
20. Shakshuka with Spinach & Feta — 17

SALADS — 18

1. Mediterranean Chickpea Salad — 19
2. Kale and Quinoa Salad — 19
3. Spinach, Avocado & Strawberry Salad — 19
4. Grilled Chicken & Mixed Salad — 19
5. Cucumber and Tomato Salad — 20
6. Roasted Beet & Goat Cheese Salad — 20
7. Quinoa & Roasted Vegetable Salad — 20
8. Shrimp and Avocado Salad — 21
9. Arugula & Watermelon Salad with Feta — 21
10. Broccoli and Cranberry Salad — 21
11. Greek Salad with Salmon — 21
12. Caprese Salad with Balsamic Glaze — 22
13. Mango and Black Bean Salad — 22
14. Spinach and Orange Salad — 22
15. Grilled Zucchini and Tomato Salad — 22
16. Tuna Salad with Avocado & Chickpeas — 23
17. Roasted Sweet Potato & Kale Salad — 23
18. Asian-Inspired Quinoa Salad — 23
19. Warm Brussels Sprout Salad — 23
20. Avocado, Grapefruit, & Shrimp Salad — 24

FISH AND SEAFOOD — 25

1. Baked Salmon with Lemon and Dill — 26
2. Garlic & Herb Grilled Shrimp Skewers — 26
3. Seared Tuna with Sesame Ginger Sauce — 26
4. Lemon Herb Baked Cod — 26
5. Spicy Grilled Salmon — 27
6. Herb-Crusted Baked Tilapia — 27
7. Teriyaki Glazed Salmon — 27
8. Coconut-Curry Shrimp Stir-Fry — 28
9. Grilled Swordfish with Mango Salsa — 28
10. Mediterranean Baked Halibut — 28
11. Lemon Garlic Butter Shrimp — 28
12. Pan-Seared Sea Bass — 29
13. Cajun-Spiced Baked Catfish — 29
14. Sesame Crusted Ahi Tuna Salad — 29
15. Pesto Grilled Scallop Skewers — 30
16. Miso-Glazed Black Cod — 30
17. Shrimp and Asparagus Stir-Fry — 30
18. Baked Haddock with Vegetables — 30
19. Codfish Ceviche with Avocado — 31
20. Grilled Sardines — 31

POULTRY — 32

1. Turmeric & Garlic Roasted Chicken — 33
2. Lemon Herb Grilled Chicken Breasts — 33
3. Cumin & Paprika Turkey Burgers — 33
4. Baked Rosemary Chicken Thighs — 33
5. Greek Yogurt Marinated Chicken — 34
6. Basil & Lemon Roasted Turkey Breast — 34
7. Coconut-Curry Chicken Stir-Fry — 34
8. Garlic & Herb Grilled Turkey — 35
9. Almond-Crusted Chicken Tenders — 35
10. Spinach & Feta Stuffed Chicken Breast — 35
11. Paprika and Thyme Roasted Quail — 35
12. Orange Glazed Grilled Chicken — 36
13. Balsamic Glazed Chicken — 36
14. Honey Mustard Roasted Chicken Wings — 36
15. Mediterranean Turkey Meatballs — 37
16. Lemon Garlic Chicken Skillet — 37
17. Pesto Chicken & Vegetable Kebabs — 37
18. Turmeric & Ginger Chicken Soup — 38
19. Rosemary & Dijon Mustard Chicken — 38
20. Chicken & Vegetable Lettuce Wraps — 38

SIDE DISHES — 39

1. Garlic Roasted Brussels Sprouts — 40
2. Lemon Herb Quinoa Pilaf — 40
3. Turmeric & Cumin Roasted Carrots — 40
4. Roasted Sweet Potato Wedges — 40
5. Grilled Asparagus with Lemon Zest — 41
6. Sauteed Kale with Garlic & Pine Nuts — 41
7. Cauliflower Rice with Herbs — 41
8. Balsamic Glazed Roasted Beets — 42
9. Ginger Sesame Broccoli Stir-Fry — 42
10. Mediterranean Zucchini Noodles — 42
11. Sweet Potatoes with Coconut Milk — 43
12. Lemon Dill Cucumber Salad — 43
13. Coconut-Cilantro Lime Rice — 43
14. Roasted Eggplant with Tahini Dressing — 43
15. Quinoa & Black Bean Bell Peppers — 44
16. Turmeric Infused Roasted Potatoes — 44
17. Spicy Garlic Sauteed Spinach — 44
18. Cabbage and Apple Slaw — 44
19. Sautéed Mushrooms with Thyme — 45
20. Grilled Artichokes with Lemon Aioli — 45

SOUPS — 46

1. Turmeric and Lentil Soup — 47
2. Ginger Carrot Soup with Coconut Milk — 47
3. Tomato Basil Quinoa Soup — 47
4. Spicy Kale & Chickpea Soup — 47
5. Lemon Garlic Chicken Soup — 48
6. Butternut Squash and Apple Soup — 48
7. Thai Coconut Shrimp Soup — 48
8. Spinach and White Bean Soup — 49
9. Broccoli and Turmeric Soup — 49
10. Moroccan Spiced Lentil Soup — 49
11. Creamy Cauliflower & Leek Soup — 49
12. Chicken and Vegetable Detox Soup — 50
13. Tom Yum Soup with Shrimp — 50
14. Quinoa Minestrone Soup — 50
15. Roasted Red Pepper & Tomato Soup — 51
16. Miso Soup with Tofu and Seaweed — 51
17. Black Bean and Vegetable Chili — 51
18. Lemon Chicken Orzo Soup — 51
19. Spiced Pumpkin Soup — 52
20. Cabbage & Turmeric Detox Soup — 52

VEGETARIAN — 53

1. Vegetable & Quinoa Stuffed Peppers — 54
2. Lentil and Sweet Potato Curry — 54
3. Chickpea & Spinach Coconut Curry — 54
4. Eggplant and Tomato Caponata — 54
5. Grilled Portobello Mushrooms — 55
6. Quinoa & Black Bean Veggie Burgers — 55
7. Spinach & Feta Stuffed Mushrooms — 55
8. Ratatouille with Herbs de Provence — 55
9. Cauliflower Steak — 56
10. Sweet Potato & Black Bean Enchiladas — 56
11. Zucchini Noodles — 56
12. Mediterranean Chickpea Patties — 57
13. Red Pepper & Spinach Quesadillas — 57
14. Wild Mushroom Risotto — 57
15. Stuffed Acorn Squash — 57
16. Spinach & Artichoke Stuffed Portobellos — 58
17. Turmeric Coconut Chickpea Stew — 58
18. Pesto Zoodles with Cherry Tomatoes — 58
19. Butternut Squash & Sage Risotto — 59
20. Greek-Style Roasted Vegetables — 59

MEAL PLAN — 60

CONVERSION TABLE — 64

BONUS — 65

What is the Anti-Inflammatory Diet?

Inflammation is a natural and essential response by the body's immune system to injury, infection, or harmful stimuli.

While acute inflammation is a short-term, localized process that aids in the healing of damaged tissues, chronic inflammation is a prolonged and systemic response that can lead to a cascade of health issues, including heart disease, arthritis, and even cancer.

The anti-inflammatory diet aims to combat chronic inflammation by promoting the consumption of foods rich in anti-inflammatory properties and minimizing those that contribute to inflammation.

Biology of Inflammation

Inflammation is your body's way of protecting itself from harm and starting the healing process. It's like a superhero response to deal with injuries, infections, or irritants. Let's break down the biology of inflammation in simpler terms:

1. The First Responder - White Blood Cells (WBCs):

- Imagine your body as a bustling city, and white blood cells are like superhero police officers. When there's trouble (like a cut or infection), these white blood cells rush to the scene to defend and fix things.

2. Signaling Molecules - Cytokines:

- Think of cytokines as messengers that tell the white blood cells where the problem is. They guide the immune system to the specific spot that needs attention.

3. The Battle Scene - Inflammation Begins:

- Picture a battle scene at the site of injury or infection. The white blood cells release substances to create a barricade, isolating the problem area. This barricade is what we often see and feel as redness, swelling, and warmth.

Examples:

- Cut or Scratch: If you accidentally cut yourself, inflammation helps by sending white blood cells to stop bleeding, fight off any potential infections, and repair the damaged tissue.
- Infection: When you get sick, like with a cold, inflammation fights off the virus or bacteria causing the infection. This is why you might experience symptoms like a runny nose or fever – it's your body's way of responding.

In summary, inflammation is like your body's superhero response team, working to fix problems and keep you healthy. It's a crucial process for survival, but when it becomes chronic, it can lead to health issues.

Understanding this biological process helps us appreciate the body's incredible ability to heal and why maintaining a balance is essential for overall well-being.

Triggers of Chronic Inflammation

Chronic inflammation can be fueled by various lifestyle factors and environmental elements. Understanding these triggers is crucial for making informed choices that support an anti-inflammatory lifestyle. Let's explore some common triggers in simple terms:

1. Poor Diet:

- *Example*: Consuming a lot of sugary snacks, processed foods, and unhealthy fats can trigger inflammation. These foods may prompt the immune system to overreact, leading to chronic inflammation.

2. Sedentary Lifestyle:

- *Example*: Sitting for long periods without enough physical activity can contribute to inflammation. Regular movement and exercise help maintain a healthy balance in the body's inflammatory responses.

3. Chronic Stress:

- *Example:* Dealing with ongoing stress at work or in personal life can trigger inflammation. The body's stress response, when persistent, may lead to chronic inflammation.

4. Lack of Sleep:

- *Example:* Not getting enough quality sleep on a regular basis can be a trigger. Adequate sleep is essential for the body to repair and regulate inflammatory processes.

5. Environmental Toxins:

- *Example:* Exposure to pollutants, chemicals, and other environmental toxins can contribute to inflammation. Being mindful of surroundings and minimizing exposure helps reduce this risk.

6. Smoking:

- *Example:* Smoking tobacco is a known trigger for inflammation. The harmful chemicals in cigarette smoke can provoke an inflammatory response in the body.

7. Excessive Alcohol Consumption:

- *Example:* Drinking alcohol in excess can contribute to inflammation. Moderation is key, as excessive alcohol intake may overstimulate the immune system.

8. Infections:

- *Example:* Persistent infections, such as untreated gum disease or chronic respiratory infections, can keep the immune system activated, leading to ongoing inflammation.

Understanding these triggers empowers individuals to make lifestyle choices that promote overall health and well-being. By addressing these factors, one can actively work towards reducing chronic inflammation and supporting the body's natural balance.

The Link Between Inflammation and Chronic Diseases

Understanding the link between inflammation and chronic diseases is crucial in appreciating the impact of inflammation on our overall health. Imagine inflammation as a double-edged sword – a necessary response to injuries and infections, but when left unchecked, it can contribute to the development and progression of various chronic conditions.

INFLAMMATION AND CARDIOVASCULAR DISEASES:

Picture your arteries as highways that carry blood throughout your body. Chronic inflammation can lead to the buildup of fatty deposits along the arterial walls, forming plaques. Over time, these plaques can narrow the arteries, increasing the risk of heart attacks and strokes. Inflammation is like a spark that ignites this process, making it a significant player in cardiovascular diseases.

INFLAMMATION AND ARTHRITIS:

Think of your joints as well-oiled machines. Chronic inflammation can disrupt this smooth operation, causing pain, swelling, and stiffness. Conditions like rheumatoid arthritis are characterized by the immune system mistakenly attacking the joints, leading to chronic inflammation. Addressing inflammation becomes pivotal in managing and preventing the progression of arthritis.

INFLAMMATION AND DIABETES:

Imagine your cells as tiny power plants that require fuel (glucose) to function. Chronic inflammation can interfere with the body's ability to use insulin efficiently, leading to insulin resistance. This disruption in the insulin-glucose balance is a key factor in the development of type 2 diabetes. Managing inflammation is, therefore, a crucial aspect of diabetes prevention and management.

INFLAMMATION AND CANCER:

Envision your cells as a bustling community with

strict rules to ensure orderly growth and division. Chronic inflammation can disrupt these rules, promoting the uncontrolled growth of cells and potentially leading to cancer. Inflammatory conditions, like inflammatory bowel disease, are associated with an increased risk of certain cancers, emphasizing the importance of mitigating chronic inflammation.

INFLAMMATION AND NEUROLOGICAL DISEASES:

Think of your brain as a complex computer system. Chronic inflammation has been linked to neurodegenerative diseases such as Alzheimer's and Parkinson's. Inflammation in the brain can contribute to the formation of abnormal protein deposits, impacting nerve cell function and communication.

Understanding these connections emphasizes the need to manage inflammation through lifestyle choices, including a diet rich in anti-inflammatory foods. By making mindful choices, we can reduce the risk of chronic diseases and promote long-term health and well-being.

Recognizing Symptoms of Inflammation

Understanding the signs that your body might be experiencing inflammation is crucial for early intervention and adopting a proactive approach to health. Here are some simple ways to recognize the symptoms of inflammation:

1. Fatigue:

- Feeling excessively tired, even after a good night's sleep.
- Struggling with energy levels throughout the day, despite minimal physical exertion.

2. Joint Pain:

- Aching or stiffness in the joints, particularly after periods of rest or inactivity.
- Discomfort that may be more pronounced during movement or after engaging in physical activities.

3. Digestive Issues:

- Occasional bloating, gas, or abdominal discomfort.
- Changes in bowel habits, such as irregularity or an increase in episodes of diarrhea or constipation.

4. Skin Problems:

- Persistent skin conditions, like eczema or psoriasis, that seem to worsen or flare up.
- Unexplained rashes or redness on the skin.

5. Allergies and Sensitivities:

- Heightened sensitivity or increased frequency of allergic reactions.
- Development of new sensitivities to foods, environmental factors, or substances.

6. Unexplained Weight Changes:

- Sudden weight gain or difficulty losing weight, despite maintaining a balanced diet and exercise routine.
- Loss of appetite or unexplained weight loss.

7. Chronic Respiratory Issues:

- Frequent or persistent respiratory problems, such as asthma or chronic bronchitis.
- Difficulty breathing or shortness of breath without an apparent cause.

8. Cognitive Challenges:

- Difficulty concentrating or "brain fog."
- Memory issues or a sense of mental cloudiness.

It's important to note that experiencing one or more of these symptoms doesn't necessarily mean inflammation is the sole cause. However, if you notice a cluster of these signs persisting over time, it may be worth consulting with a healthcare professional to explore potential underlying causes, including chronic inflammation.

Taking note of these symptoms allows for early detection and the implementation of lifestyle changes, such as adopting an anti-inflammatory diet, to promote overall well-being.

Lifestyle: Finding Balance for Well-being

Inflammation isn't just about what you eat; it's influenced by how you live. Your daily habits can either fan the flames of inflammation or douse them. Let's explore how lifestyle choices play a crucial role:

1. SLEEP: THE RESTORATION PERIOD

Imagine sleep as your body's nightly repair shop. Lack of sleep or poor sleep quality disrupts this repair process, leading to increased inflammation. Aim for 7-9 hours of quality sleep each night to give your body the restoration it needs.

Tip: Create a calming bedtime routine, limit screen time before sleep, and keep your bedroom cool and dark.

2. PHYSICAL ACTIVITY: MOVE TO SOOTHE

Regular exercise isn't just for weight management; it's a potent inflammation regulator. Moderate exercise, like brisk walking or cycling, helps reduce inflammation. On the flip side, excessive, intense exercise without proper recovery may do the opposite.

Tip: Find an activity you enjoy, whether it's dancing, hiking, or yoga, and aim for at least 150 minutes of moderate exercise per week.

3. STRESS MANAGEMENT: RELAX AND REBALANCE

Stress triggers the release of hormones that can fuel inflammation. Chronic stress keeps these hormones elevated, promoting inflammation over time. Incorporate stress-reducing activities into your routine, like mindfulness, deep breathing, or spending time in nature.

Tip: Practice mindfulness techniques, take short breaks during the day, and engage in activities that bring joy and relaxation.

4. SMOKING AND INFLAMMATION: A HARMFUL DUO

Smoking is like throwing gasoline on the inflammatory fire. It not only damages your lungs but also contributes to systemic inflammation, increasing the risk of various diseases.

Tip: Seek support to quit smoking, whether through counseling, support groups, or nicotine replacement therapies.

5. ALCOHOL MODERATION: TOAST TO HEALTH, NOT INFLAMMATION

While some studies suggest moderate alcohol consumption may have anti-inflammatory effects, excessive drinking can lead to inflammation and damage organs. Stick to moderate levels – one drink per day for women and up to two drinks per day for men.

Tip: Know your limits and choose lower-alcohol beverages like red wine, which contains antioxidants.

Remember, it's the combination of these lifestyle factors that creates a harmonious, anti-inflammatory environment within your body. Small, consistent changes can make a big difference in taming inflammation and promoting overall well-being.

Benefits of an Anti-Inflammatory Diet

Embracing an anti-inflammatory diet brings a multitude of health benefits, offering a natural and delicious way to support your overall well-being. Let's explore some of the key advantages in simple terms:

1. Improved Heart Health:

- *Explanation:* An anti-inflammatory diet can help keep your heart happy by reducing levels of inflammation in blood vessels.
- *Example:* Consuming omega-3-rich fish like salmon or incorporating flaxseeds into your diet helps lower inflammation, promoting a healthier heart.

2. Joint Pain Relief:

- *Explanation:* By minimizing inflammation, an anti-inflammatory diet can ease discomfort in your joints and muscles.
- *Example:* Adding turmeric, a natural

anti-inflammatory spice, to your meals can contribute to reduced joint pain and increased mobility.

3. Enhanced Digestive Health:

- *Explanation:* An anti-inflammatory diet supports a gut-friendly environment, promoting better digestion and absorption of nutrients.
- *Example:* Including fiber-rich foods like vegetables, fruits, and whole grains supports a diverse and healthy gut microbiome.

4. Weight Management:

- *Explanation:* Chronic inflammation can contribute to weight gain, and an anti-inflammatory diet can aid in weight management.
- *Example:* Choosing nutrient-dense foods over processed options helps regulate appetite and supports a healthy weight.

5. Reduced Risk of Chronic Diseases:

- *Explanation:* Chronic inflammation is linked to diseases like diabetes, Alzheimer's, and certain cancers. An anti-inflammatory diet can lower this risk.
- *Example:* Consuming antioxidant-rich foods, such as berries and leafy greens, helps combat oxidative stress and reduces the risk of chronic diseases.

6. Balanced Blood Sugar Levels:

- *Explanation:* An anti-inflammatory diet can assist in maintaining stable blood sugar levels, crucial for overall health.
- *Example:* Opting for complex carbohydrates like sweet potatoes instead of refined sugars helps prevent spikes and crashes in blood sugar.

7. Enhanced Mood and Mental Clarity:

- *Explanation:* Chronic inflammation can impact mental health. An anti-inflammatory diet supports a healthy brain and may positively affect mood.
- *Example:* Consuming fatty fish with omega-3s, like mackerel or sardines, supports brain health and may contribute to improved mood.

Incorporating these simple dietary changes not only helps fight inflammation but also contributes to a happier, healthier you. The benefits extend beyond physical well-being, positively impacting various aspects of your life.

Key Principles and Guidelines

Adopting an anti-inflammatory diet involves embracing certain principles and guidelines to promote overall health and reduce chronic inflammation.
Let's explore these key principles in simple terms, along with practical examples:

1. Choose Whole, Unprocessed Foods:

- **Principle:** Opt for foods in their natural state, minimizing processed and refined options.
- **Example:** Instead of sugary breakfast cereals, go for whole oats topped with fresh berries and a sprinkle of nuts.

2. Prioritize Fruits and Vegetables:

- **Principle:** Load up on colorful fruits and vegetables rich in antioxidants and anti-inflammatory compounds.
- **Example:** Make a vibrant salad with leafy greens, tomatoes, cucumbers, and bell peppers as a side dish or a main meal.

3. Include Omega-3 Fatty Acids:

- **Principle:** Incorporate sources of omega-3s, known for their anti-inflammatory properties.
- **Example:** Enjoy fatty fish like salmon or mackerel twice a week, or sprinkle chia seeds on your morning yogurt or oatmeal.

4. Embrace Healthy Fats:

- **Principle:** Choose monounsaturated and polyunsaturated fats over saturated and trans fats.
- **Example:** Use olive oil for cooking and as a salad dressing, and snack on a handful of almonds instead of chips.

5. Opt for Lean Proteins:

- **Principle:** Select lean protein sources to support muscle health and reduce inflammation.

- **Example:** Grill or bake chicken or turkey breast instead of processed meats like sausages or bacon.

6. Limit Added Sugars:

- **Principle:** Reduce intake of added sugars, which can contribute to inflammation.
- **Example:** Choose water or herbal tea over sugary sodas, and satisfy your sweet tooth with fresh fruit or a small piece of dark chocolate.

7. Watch Your Portions:

- **Principle:** Be mindful of portion sizes to maintain a healthy weight and prevent overeating.
- **Example:** Use smaller plates to help control portion sizes and avoid going back for seconds out of habit.

8. Stay Hydrated with Water:

- **Principle:** Hydrate your body with water, a crucial component for overall health.
- **Example:** Carry a reusable water bottle and aim to drink at least 8 glasses of water throughout the day.

9. Experiment with Anti-Inflammatory Spices:

- **Principle:** Incorporate spices known for their anti-inflammatory properties, such as turmeric and ginger.
- **Example:** Add turmeric to soups, stews, or a morning smoothie, and use fresh ginger in stir-fries or tea.

By following these simple principles, you can create a balanced and anti-inflammatory eating pattern that promotes wellness and supports your body's natural defense against chronic inflammation.

Foods to Include and Avoid

Include more:

Food Group	Specific Foods	Reasons to Include
Fatty Fish	Salmon, Mackerel, Sardines, Trout	Rich in omega-3 fatty acids, known for their potent anti-inflammatory properties.
Leafy Greens	Spinach, Kale, Swiss Chard, Collard Greens	High in antioxidants, vitamins, and minerals that combat inflammation.
Berries	Blueberries, Strawberries, Raspberries	Packed with antioxidants and fiber, aiding in reducing inflammation.
Nuts and Seeds	Almonds, Walnuts, Chia Seeds, Flaxseeds	Provide healthy fats, fiber, and essential nutrients with anti-inflammatory effects.
Whole Grains	Quinoa, Brown Rice, Oats, Barley	Complex carbohydrates with fiber and nutrients, supporting a balanced diet.
Healthy Oils	Olive Oil, Avocado Oil, Flaxseed Oil	Rich in monounsaturated fats and omega-3 fatty acids, beneficial for inflammation.
Turmeric and Ginger	Fresh Turmeric, Ground Turmeric, Fresh Ginger	Contains curcumin and gingerol, powerful anti-inflammatory compounds.
Colorful Vegetables	Bell Peppers, Tomatoes, Broccoli, Carrots	Provide a variety of antioxidants and phytonutrients that fight inflammation.
Legumes	Lentils, Chickpeas, Black Beans, Kidney Beans	Excellent plant-based protein sources with anti-inflammatory properties.
Green Tea	Unsweetened Green Tea	Contains catechins, known for their antioxidant and anti-inflammatory effects.
Probiotic-Rich Foods	Yogurt (with live cultures), Kefir, Kimchi	Support gut health, influencing inflammation and overall wellbeing.

Avoid or limit:

Food Group	Specific Foods	Reasons to Include
Processed Foods	Packaged Snacks, Fast Food, Frozen Meals	Often high in unhealthy fats, sugars, and additives that can contribute to inflammation.
Refined Sugars	Candy, Soda, Pastries, Sugary Cereals	High sugar intake is linked to increased inflammation and various health issues.
Red and Processed Meats	Beef, Pork, Bacon, Sausages, Processed Meats	Associated with higher levels of inflammation and may contribute to chronic diseases.
Fried Foods	French Fries, Fried Chicken, Onion Rings	High in unhealthy fats, promoting inflammation and overall health risks.
Saturated and Trans Fats	Butter, Margarine, Processed Snacks	Found in certain oils and processed foods, contributing to inflammation and heart issues.
Excessive Alcohol	Alcoholic Beverages	Excessive alcohol consumption can trigger inflammation and negatively impact health.
White Flour and White Bread	White Bread, Pastries, White Pasta	Lack fiber and essential nutrients, potentially promoting inflammation.
Artificial Additives and Preservatives	Processed Foods, Ready Meals, Sugary Drinks	May have inflammatory effects and negatively impact overall health.
High-Processed Dairy Products	Processed Cheese, Sweetened Yogurts	Some individuals may experience inflammation with high intake of processed dairy.
Excessive Red and Processed Meats	Steaks, Hot Dogs, Deli Meats	Linked to increased inflammation and higher risks of chronic diseases.
High Sodium Foods	Processed Foods, Salty Snacks, Canned Soups	Excessive salt intake can contribute to inflammation and other health concerns.

Including a variety of anti-inflammatory foods while minimizing or avoiding pro-inflammatory ones can contribute to better overall health and well-being.

Breakfast

1. Turmeric Scrambled Eggs with Spinach

Preparation time: 10 minutes
Servings: 2

Ingredients:

- 4 large eggs
- 1 cup fresh spinach, chopped
- 1/2 teaspoon ground turmeric
- Salt and pepper to taste
- Olive oil for cooking

Instructions:

1. In a bowl, whisk the eggs and add turmeric, salt, and pepper. Mix well.
2. Heat olive oil in a pan over medium heat.
3. Add chopped spinach to the pan and sauté until wilted.
4. Pour the egg mixture over the spinach and stir gently.
5. Cook the eggs, stirring occasionally until they are scrambled to your liking.
6. Serve immediately and enjoy the golden goodness!

Nutritional Information (per serving):
Cal: 190 | Carbs: 2g | Pro: 15g | Fat: 13g
Sugars: 1g | Fiber: 1g

2. Quinoa Breakfast Bowl

Preparation time: 15 minutes
Servings: 2

Ingredients:

- 1 cup cooked quinoa
- 1 cup mixed berries (strawberries, blueberries, raspberries)
- 1/4 cup almonds, chopped
- 2 tablespoons honey (optional)
- Greek yogurt for topping (optional)

Instructions:

1. Divide cooked quinoa between two bowls.
2. Top with mixed berries and chopped almonds.
3. Drizzle honey over the bowl if desired.
4. Add a dollop of Greek yogurt on top for extra creaminess (optional).
5. Mix well and savor the delightful blend of flavors.

Nutritional Information (per serving):
Cal: 320 | Carbs: 50g | Pro: 9g | Fat: 10g
Sugars: 17g | Fiber: 8g

3. Avocado Toast with Salmon

Preparation time: 5 minutes
Servings: 2

Ingredients:

- 2 slices whole-grain bread, toasted
- 1 ripe avocado, mashed
- 4 oz smoked salmon
- Lemon juice (optional)
- Fresh dill for garnish (optional)

Instructions:

1. Toast the whole-grain bread slices to your liking.
2. Spread mashed avocado evenly on each slice.
3. Top with smoked salmon, arranging it to cover the avocado.
4. Squeeze a bit of lemon juice over the salmon for extra freshness (optional).
5. Garnish with fresh dill if desired.
6. Enjoy this simple yet luxurious breakfast!

Nutritional Information (per serving):
Cal: 290 | Carbs: 25g | Pro: 15g | Fat: 15g
Sugars: 2g | Fiber: 8g

4. Chia Seed Pudding with Berries

Preparation time: 5 minutes (plus chilling time)
Servings: 2

Ingredients:

- 1/4 cup chia seeds
- 1 cup almond milk (or any preferred milk)
- 1 tablespoon maple syrup (optional)
- 1/2 teaspoon vanilla extract
- Mixed berries for topping

Instructions:

1. In a bowl, combine chia seeds, almond milk, maple syrup (if using), and vanilla extract.
2. Stir well, ensuring the chia seeds are fully submerged.
3. Cover and refrigerate for at least 3 hours or

overnight.
4. Once the pudding has set, divide it into two servings.
5. Top with a generous amount of mixed berries.
6. Indulge in a delightful and nutrient-packed chia seed pudding.

Nutritional Information (per serving):
Cal: 150 | Carbs: 20g | Pro: 4g | Fat: 7g
Sugars: 7g | Fiber: 10g

5. Oatmeal with Walnuts & Blueberries

Preparation time: 10 minutes
Servings: 2

Ingredients:

- 1 cup old-fashioned oats
- 2 cups water or milk of choice
- 1/4 cup walnuts, chopped
- 1/2 cup blueberries
- Honey or maple syrup for sweetness (optional)

Instructions:

1. In a saucepan, bring water or milk to a boil.
2. Stir in the old-fashioned oats and reduce heat to simmer.
3. Cook the oats until they reach your desired consistency.
4. Divide the cooked oats between two bowls.
5. Top with chopped walnuts and fresh blueberries.
6. Drizzle with honey or maple syrup for added sweetness if desired.
7. Enjoy a heartwarming bowl of nourishing oatmeal.

Nutritional Information (per serving):
Cal: 270 | Carbs: 43g | Pro: 8g | Fat: 9g
Sugars: 9g | Fiber: 7g

6. Sweet Potato and Kale Hash

Preparation time: 20 minutes
Servings: 2

Ingredients:

- 1 large sweet potato, diced
- 1 cup kale, chopped
- 1 tablespoon olive oil
- 2 eggs
- Salt and pepper to taste

Instructions:

1. In a skillet, heat olive oil over medium heat.
2. Add diced sweet potatoes and cook until they begin to soften.
3. Stir in chopped kale and cook until both are tender.
4. Create two wells in the mixture and crack an egg into each.
5. Cook until the eggs are done to your liking.
6. Season with salt and pepper to taste.
7. Serve this hearty breakfast hash for a nutrient-packed start to your day.

Nutritional Information (per serving):
Cal: 280 | Carbs: 38g | Pro: 8g | Fat: 11g
Sugars: 7g | Fiber: 7g

7. Greek Yogurt Parfait

Preparation time: 5 minutes
Servings: 2

Ingredients:

- 1 cup Greek yogurt
- 1/2 cup granola (choose a low-sugar option)
- 1 ripe mango, diced
- Honey for drizzling (optional)
- Fresh mint for garnish (optional)

Instructions:

1. In two glasses or bowls, layer Greek yogurt at the bottom.
2. Add a layer of granola on top of the yogurt.
3. Top with diced mango.
4. Repeat the layers until the glasses are filled.
5. Drizzle with honey for sweetness if desired.
6. Garnish with fresh mint for a burst of flavor (optional).
7. Delight in the creamy and refreshing Greek yogurt parfait.

Nutritional Information (per serving):
Cal: 320 | Carbs: 49g | Pro: 16g | Fat: 8g
Sugars: 29g | Fiber: 4g

8. Salmon and Spinach Omelette

Preparation time: 15 minutes

Servings: 2

Ingredients:

- 4 large eggs
- 1/2 cup cooked salmon, flaked
- 1 cup fresh spinach
- Salt and pepper to taste
- Olive oil for cooking

Instructions:

1. In a bowl, whisk the eggs and season with salt and pepper.
2. Heat olive oil in a non-stick skillet over medium heat.
3. Add fresh spinach to the skillet and sauté until wilted.
4. Pour the whisked eggs over the spinach.
5. Sprinkle flaked salmon evenly over the eggs.
6. Allow the omelette to cook, folding it in half when the eggs are set.
7. Serve hot, with an extra sprinkle of pepper if desired.
8. Enjoy a protein-packed salmon and spinach omelette.

Nutritional Information (per serving):
Cal: 260 | Carbs: 2g | Pro: 28g | Fat: 16g
Sugars: 0g | Fiber: 1g

9. Green Smoothie Bowl

Preparation time: 10 minutes
Servings: 2

Ingredients:

- 2 cups fresh kale, stems removed
- 1 cup pineapple chunks (fresh or frozen)
- 1 banana
- 1/2 cup almond milk (or any preferred milk)
- Toppings: Sliced kiwi, chia seeds, coconut flakes

Instructions:

1. In a blender, combine kale, pineapple, banana, and almond milk.
2. Blend until smooth, adding more liquid if needed.
3. Divide the green smoothie into two bowls.
4. Top each bowl with sliced kiwi, chia seeds, and coconut flakes.
5. Feel the refreshing burst of energy with this vibrant smoothie bowl.

Nutritional Information (per serving):
Cal: 220 | Carbs: 50g | Pro: 4g | Fat: 3g
Sugars: 27g | Fiber: 8g

10. Almond Flour Pancakes

Preparation time: 20 minutes
Servings: 2

Ingredients:

- 1 cup almond flour
- 2 large eggs
- 1/2 cup almond milk (or any preferred milk)
- 1 teaspoon baking powder
- Mixed berries for topping

Instructions:

1. In a bowl, whisk together almond flour, eggs, almond milk, and baking powder.
2. Heat a non-stick skillet over medium heat.
3. Pour small amounts of batter onto the skillet to form pancakes.
4. Cook until bubbles appear on the surface, then flip and cook the other side.
5. Stack the almond flour pancakes on a plate.
6. Top with a generous serving of mixed berries.
7. Drizzle with honey or maple syrup if desired.
8. Savor the fluffy goodness of almond flour pancakes.

Nutritional Information (per serving):
Cal: 380 | Carbs: 20g | Pro: 15g | Fat: 28g
Sugars: 7g | Fiber: 7g

11. Coconut and Berry Overnight Oats

Preparation time: 10 minutes (plus overnight soaking)
Servings: 2

Ingredients:

- 1 cup rolled oats
- 1 cup unsweetened coconut milk
- 1/2 cup mixed berries (blueberries, strawberries, raspberries)
- 2 tablespoons shredded coconut
- 1 tablespoon chia seeds

Instructions:

1. In a jar or container, combine rolled oats, coconut milk, mixed berries, shredded coconut, and chia seeds.
2. Stir the ingredients until well combined.
3. Seal the jar or container and refrigerate overnight or for at least 4 hours to allow the oats to soak and flavors to meld.
4. Before serving, give the mixture a good stir. If it's too thick, you can add a splash of coconut milk.
5. Top with additional berries and shredded coconut, if desired.

Nutritional Information (per serving):
Cal: 380 | Carbs: 46g | Pro: 9g | Fat: 18g
Sugars: 5g | Fiber: 10g

12. Veggie Frittata with Turmeric

Preparation time: 15 minutes
Servings: 2

Ingredients:

- 4 large eggs
- 1/2 cup cherry tomatoes, halved
- 1/2 cup spinach, chopped
- 1/2 teaspoon ground turmeric
- Salt and pepper to taste

Instructions:

1. Preheat the oven broiler.
2. In a bowl, beat the eggs and season with turmeric, salt, and pepper.
3. Heat an oven-safe skillet over medium heat.
4. Add cherry tomatoes and spinach to the skillet, sautéing until spinach wilts.
5. Pour the beaten eggs over the vegetables in the skillet.
6. Cook on the stovetop for 3-4 minutes until the edges set.
7. Transfer the skillet to the broiler and cook for an additional 3-4 minutes until the top is set and slightly golden.
8. Slice and serve.

Nutritional Information (per serving):
Cal: 220 | Carbs: 6g | Pro: 15g | Fat: 15g
Sugars: 2g | Fiber: 2g

13. Buckwheat Pancakes

Preparation time: 20 minutes
Servings: 2

Ingredients:

- 1 cup buckwheat flour
- 1 cup almond milk
- 1 egg
- 1 teaspoon baking powder
- Greek yogurt for serving

Instructions:

1. In a bowl, mix buckwheat flour, almond milk, egg, and baking powder until well combined.
2. Heat a non-stick skillet over medium heat.
3. Pour 1/4 cup of the batter onto the skillet for each pancake.
4. Cook until bubbles form on the surface, then flip and cook the other side.
5. Repeat until all the batter is used.
6. Serve pancakes topped with a dollop of Greek yogurt.

Nutritional Information (per serving):
Cal: 340 | Carbs: 55g | Pro: 13g | Fat: 8g
Sugars: 2g | Fiber: 10g

14. Banana Walnut Muffins

Preparation time: 15 minutes
Servings: 2 (6 muffins each)

Ingredients:

- 2 ripe bananas, mashed
- 1 cup almond flour
- 1/4 cup chopped walnuts
- 2 eggs
- 2 tablespoons ground flaxseeds

Instructions:

1. Preheat the oven to 350°F (175°C) and line a muffin tin with paper liners.
2. In a bowl, combine mashed bananas, almond flour, chopped walnuts, eggs, and ground flaxseeds. Mix well.
3. Divide the batter among the muffin cups.
4. Bake for 20-25 minutes or until a toothpick inserted comes out clean.
5. Allow the muffins to cool before serving.

Nutritional Information (per serving):
Cal: 280 | Carbs: 22g | Pro: 10g | Fat: 19g

Sugars: 8g | Fiber: 6g

15. Spinach and Mushroom Wrap

Preparation time: 10 minutes
Servings: 2

Ingredients:

- 4 whole-grain tortillas
- 1 cup spinach leaves
- 1 cup mushrooms, sliced
- 4 eggs, scrambled
- Salt and pepper to taste

Instructions:

1. In a non-stick skillet, sauté mushrooms until tender.
2. Add spinach to the skillet and cook until wilted.
3. In a separate pan, scramble the eggs.
4. Warm the tortillas in a dry skillet or microwave.
5. Divide the scrambled eggs among the tortillas, top with sautéed mushrooms and spinach.
6. Season with salt and pepper to taste.
7. Fold the sides of the tortillas and roll them up into wraps.

Nutritional Information (per serving):
Cal: 320 | Carbs: 33g | Pro: 18g | Fat: 14g
Sugars: 2g | Fiber: 6g

16. Quinoa Porridge Cinnamon Apples

Preparation time: 15 minutes
Servings: 2

Ingredients:

- 1 cup cooked quinoa
- 1 cup almond milk
- 1 apple, diced
- 1 teaspoon ground cinnamon
- 1 tablespoon honey (optional)

Instructions:

1. In a saucepan, combine cooked quinoa and almond milk.
2. Heat over medium heat until warmed through.
3. Stir in diced apples and ground cinnamon.
4. Continue to cook until the apples are softened.
5. Sweeten with honey if desired.
6. Divide into bowls and serve warm.

Nutritional Information (per serving):
Cal: 250 | Carbs: 46g | Pro: 6g | Fat: 5g
Sugars: 16g | Fiber: 7g

17. Blueberry and Almond Smoothie

Preparation time: 5 minutes
Servings: 2

Ingredients:

- 1 cup blueberries (fresh or frozen)
- 1 banana
- 1 cup almond milk
- 2 tablespoons almond butter
- Ice cubes (optional)

Instructions:

1. In a blender, combine blueberries, banana, almond milk, and almond butter.
2. Blend until smooth and creamy.
3. Add ice cubes if a colder consistency is desired.
4. Pour into glasses and serve immediately.

Nutritional Information (per serving):
Cal: 250 | Carbs: 32g | Pro: 5g | Fat: 13g
Sugars: 16g | Fiber: 6g

18. Smashed Avocado & Tomato Toast

Preparation time: 5 minutes
Servings: 2

Ingredients:

- 1 ripe avocado
- 1 large tomato, sliced
- 2 slices whole grain bread, toasted
- Salt and pepper to taste
- Red pepper flakes (optional)

Instructions:

1. Scoop out the avocado into a bowl and smash it with a fork.
2. Spread the smashed avocado evenly onto

the toasted whole grain bread slices.
3. Arrange tomato slices on top of the avocado.
4. Season with salt, pepper, and red pepper flakes if desired.
5. Serve immediately.

Nutritional Information (per serving):
Cal: 220 | Carbs: 23g | Pro: 5g | Fat: 14g
Sugars: 2g | Fiber: 7g

19. Berry Protein Smoothie

Preparation time: 5 minutes
Servings: 2

Ingredients:

- 1 cup mixed berries (strawberries, blueberries, raspberries)
- 1 cup almond milk
- 1 scoop plant-based protein powder
- 2 tablespoons hemp seeds
- Ice cubes (optional)

Instructions:

1. In a blender, combine mixed berries, almond milk, protein powder, and hemp seeds.
2. Blend until smooth.
3. Add ice cubes if desired for a colder texture.
4. Pour into glasses and enjoy immediately.

Nutritional Information (per serving):
Cal: 220 | Carbs: 20g | Pro: 20g | Fat: 8g
Sugars: 8g | Fiber: 6g

20. Shakshuka with Spinach & Feta

Preparation time: 15 minutes
Servings: 2

Ingredients:

- 4 large eggs
- 1 can (14 oz) diced tomatoes
- 1 cup fresh spinach
- 1/2 cup crumbled feta cheese
- 1 teaspoon ground cumin
- Salt and pepper to taste

Instructions:

1. In a skillet, heat diced tomatoes over medium heat.
2. Add ground cumin, salt, and pepper to the tomatoes.
3. Stir in fresh spinach and let it wilt.
4. Make wells in the tomato mixture and crack the eggs into them.
5. Cover and simmer until the eggs are cooked to your liking.
6. Sprinkle crumbled feta on top.
7. Serve hot with whole grain toast.

Nutritional Information (per serving):
Cal: 320 | Carbs: 15g | Pro: 18g | Fat: 22g
Sugars: 8g | Fiber: 4g

Salads

1. Mediterranean Chickpea Salad

Preparation time: 15 minutes
Servings: 2

Ingredients:

- 1 can (15 oz) chickpeas, drained and rinsed
- 1 cup cherry tomatoes, halved
- 1/2 cucumber, diced
- 2 oz feta cheese, crumbled
- 2 tbsp extra virgin olive oil
- Salt and pepper, to taste

Instructions:

1. In a large bowl, combine chickpeas, cherry tomatoes, cucumber, and feta cheese.
2. Drizzle extra virgin olive oil over the salad, ensuring even coating.
3. Gently toss the ingredients until well combined.
4. Season with salt and pepper to taste.
5. Serve immediately or refrigerate for a refreshing chilled salad.

Nutritional Information (per serving):
Cal: 375 | Carbs: 35g | Pro: 13g | Fat: 22g
Sugars: 7g | Fiber: 10g

2. Kale and Quinoa Salad

Preparation time: 20 minutes
Servings: 2

Ingredients:

- 1 cup cooked quinoa, cooled
- 2 cups kale, stems removed and finely chopped
- 1/2 cup pomegranate seeds
- 2 tbsp olive oil
- 1 tbsp balsamic vinegar
- Salt and pepper, to taste

Instructions:

1. In a large bowl, combine cooked quinoa, chopped kale, and pomegranate seeds.
2. In a small bowl, whisk together olive oil and balsamic vinegar.
3. Drizzle the dressing over the salad and toss until well combined.
4. Season with salt and pepper to taste.
5. Allow the flavors to meld for a few minutes before serving.

Nutritional Information (per serving):
Cal: 320 | Carbs: 39g | Pro: 7g | Fat: 16g
Sugars: 7g | Fiber: 6g

3. Spinach, Avocado & Strawberry Salad

Preparation time: 10 minutes
Servings: 2

Ingredients:

- 3 cups fresh spinach leaves
- 1 ripe avocado, sliced
- 1 cup strawberries, hulled and halved
- 2 tbsp balsamic glaze
- 1 tbsp extra virgin olive oil
- Salt and pepper, to taste

Instructions:

1. In a large bowl, combine fresh spinach, avocado slices, and halved strawberries.
2. Drizzle balsamic glaze and extra virgin olive oil over the salad.
3. Toss gently until ingredients are evenly coated.
4. Season with salt and pepper to taste.
5. Serve immediately for optimal freshness.

Nutritional Information (per serving):
Cal: 275 | Carbs: 20g | Pro: 4g | Fat: 21g
Sugars: 7g | Fiber: 9g

4. Grilled Chicken & Mixed Salad

Preparation time: 15 minutes
Servings: 2

Ingredients:

- 2 boneless, skinless chicken breasts
- 6 cups mixed salad greens
- 1 cup cherry tomatoes, halved
- 2 tbsp balsamic vinaigrette
- 1 tbsp olive oil
- Salt and pepper, to taste

Instructions:

1. Season chicken breasts with salt and pepper.
2. Grill chicken until fully cooked, approximately 6-8 minutes per side.

3. In a large bowl, toss mixed greens and cherry tomatoes.
4. Slice grilled chicken and place on top of the salad.
5. Drizzle with balsamic vinaigrette and olive oil.
6. Toss gently and serve immediately.

Nutritional Information (per serving):
Cal: 385 | Carbs: 12g | Pro: 36g | Fat: 21g
Sugars: 6g | Fiber: 4g

5. Cucumber and Tomato Salad

Preparation time: 10 minutes
Servings: 2

Ingredients:

- 2 large cucumbers, sliced
- 1 cup cherry tomatoes, halved
- 2 tbsp extra virgin olive oil
- 1 tbsp red wine vinegar
- 1 tsp dried oregano
- Salt and pepper, to taste

Instructions:

1. In a bowl, combine cucumber slices and cherry tomatoes.
2. In a small bowl, whisk together olive oil, red wine vinegar, and dried oregano.
3. Drizzle the dressing over the cucumber and tomato mixture.
4. Toss gently until all ingredients are well coated.
5. Season with salt and pepper to taste.
6. Allow the salad to marinate for a few minutes before serving.

Nutritional Information (per serving):
Cal: 150 | Carbs: 10g | Pro: 2g | Fat: 12g
Sugars: 4g | Fiber: 3g

6. Roasted Beet & Goat Cheese Salad

Preparation time: 30 minutes
Servings: 2

Ingredients:

- 2 medium-sized beets, peeled and diced
- 2 cups mixed salad greens
- 2 oz goat cheese, crumbled
- 2 tbsp balsamic glaze
- 1 tbsp walnut oil
- Salt and pepper, to taste

Instructions:

1. Preheat the oven to 400°F (200°C).
2. Toss diced beets with walnut oil, salt, and pepper.
3. Roast beets in the oven for 20-25 minutes or until tender.
4. In a bowl, combine mixed salad greens and roasted beets.
5. Crumble goat cheese over the salad.
6. Drizzle with balsamic glaze and toss gently.
7. Serve immediately, allowing the warmth of the beets to slightly melt the goat cheese.

Nutritional Information (per serving):
Cal: 240 | Carbs: 18g | Pro: 8g | Fat: 16g
Sugars: 9g | Fiber: 5g

7. Quinoa & Roasted Vegetable Salad

Preparation time: 25 minutes
Servings: 2

Ingredients:

- 1 cup cooked quinoa, cooled
- 1 zucchini, diced
- 1 red bell pepper, sliced
- 1 cup cherry tomatoes, halved
- 2 tbsp balsamic vinaigrette
- 1 tbsp olive oil
- Salt and pepper, to taste

Instructions:

1. Preheat the oven to 400°F (200°C).
2. Toss diced zucchini, sliced red bell pepper, and cherry tomatoes with olive oil, salt, and pepper.
3. Roast vegetables in the oven for 15-20 minutes or until tender.
4. In a bowl, combine cooked quinoa and roasted vegetables.
5. Drizzle with balsamic vinaigrette and toss gently.
6. Season with additional salt and pepper if needed.
7. Serve warm or at room temperature.

Nutritional Information (per serving):
Cal: 315 | Carbs: 42g | Pro: 8g | Fat: 13g
Sugars: 7g | Fiber: 7g

8. Shrimp and Avocado Salad

Preparation time: 15 minutes
Servings: 2

Ingredients:

- 1/2 lb shrimp, peeled and deveined
- 1 avocado, diced
- 2 cups mixed salad greens
- 2 tbsp lime juice
- 1 tbsp olive oil
- Salt and pepper, to taste

Instructions:

1. Season shrimp with salt and pepper.
2. In a skillet over medium heat, cook shrimp until opaque (about 2-3 minutes per side).
3. In a large bowl, combine mixed salad greens, diced avocado, and cooked shrimp.
4. In a small bowl, whisk together lime juice and olive oil.
5. Drizzle the lime dressing over the salad and toss gently.
6. Serve immediately for a fresh and vibrant salad.

Nutritional Information (per serving):
Cal: 275 | Carbs: 9g | Pro: 23g | Fat: 18g
Sugars: 1g | Fiber: 6g

9. Arugula & Watermelon Salad with Feta

Preparation time: 15 minutes
Servings: 2

Ingredients:

- 4 cups arugula
- 1 cup watermelon, cubed
- 2 oz feta cheese, crumbled
- 2 tbsp balsamic glaze
- 1 tbsp extra virgin olive oil
- Salt and pepper, to taste

Instructions:

1. In a large bowl, combine arugula, watermelon cubes, crumbled feta cheese.
2. Drizzle with balsamic glaze and extra virgin olive oil.
3. Toss gently until ingredients are evenly coated.
4. Season with salt and pepper to taste.
5. Serve immediately for a refreshing and sweet-savory combination.

Nutritional Information (per serving):
Cal: 190 | Carbs: 12g | Pro: 6g | Fat: 14g
Sugars: 8g | Fiber: 2g

10. Broccoli and Cranberry Salad

Preparation time: 20 minutes
Servings: 2

Ingredients:

- 2 cups broccoli florets, blanched
- 1/2 cup dried cranberries
- 1/4 cup almonds, sliced
- 2 tbsp olive oil
- 1 tbsp apple cider vinegar
- Salt and pepper, to taste

Instructions:

1. In a bowl, combine blanched broccoli florets, dried cranberries, and sliced almonds.
2. In a small bowl, whisk together olive oil and apple cider vinegar.
3. Drizzle the dressing over the salad and toss gently.
4. Season with salt and pepper to taste.
5. Allow the salad to marinate for a few minutes before serving.

Nutritional Information (per serving):
Cal: 240 | Carbs: 23g | Pro: 4g | Fat: 16g
Sugars: 11g | Fiber: 6g

11. Greek Salad with Salmon

Preparation time: 15 minutes
Servings: 2

Ingredients:

- 8 oz (about 225g) salmon fillet, grilled and flaked
- 2 cups cherry tomatoes, halved
- 1 cucumber, diced
- 1/2 red onion, thinly sliced
- 1 cup Kalamata olives, pitted
- 1 cup feta cheese, crumbled
- Fresh oregano for garnish (optional)

Instructions:

1. In a large bowl, combine the grilled and flaked salmon, halved cherry tomatoes, diced cucumber, thinly sliced red onion, pitted Kalamata olives, crumbled feta cheese.
2. Toss the ingredients gently to combine.
3. Garnish with fresh oregano if desired.
4. Serve immediately, and enjoy this refreshing Greek Salad with Salmon!

Nutritional Information (per serving):
Cal: 498 | Carbs: 16g | Pro: 36g | Fat: 34g
Sugars: 8g | Fiber: 4g

12. Caprese Salad with Balsamic Glaze

Preparation time: 10 minutes
Servings: 2

Ingredients:

- 2 large tomatoes, sliced
- 1 ball fresh mozzarella, sliced
- Fresh basil leaves
- Balsamic glaze
- Olive oil for drizzling

Instructions:

1. Arrange alternating slices of tomatoes and fresh mozzarella on a serving plate.
2. Tuck fresh basil leaves between the tomato and mozzarella slices.
3. Drizzle with balsamic glaze and olive oil.
4. Serve immediately and enjoy the simplicity of this Caprese Salad!

Nutritional Information (per serving):
Cal: 315 | Carbs: 8g | Pro: 18g | Fat: 25g
Sugars: 4g | Fiber: 2g

13. Mango and Black Bean Salad

Preparation time: 15 minutes
Servings: 2

Ingredients:

- 1 ripe mango, diced
- 1 can (15 oz) black beans, drained and rinsed
- 1/2 red onion, finely chopped
- 1/4 cup fresh cilantro, chopped
- Juice of 2 limes

Instructions:

1. In a large bowl, combine diced mango, black beans, chopped red onion, and fresh cilantro.
2. Squeeze the juice of 2 limes over the ingredients.
3. Toss gently to mix.
4. Serve immediately and enjoy this vibrant Mango and Black Bean Salad!

Nutritional Information (per serving):
Cal: 280 | Carbs: 57g | Pro: 14g | Fat: 1g
Sugars: 19g | Fiber: 15g

14. Spinach and Orange Salad

Preparation time: 10 minutes
Servings: 2

Ingredients:

- 4 cups baby spinach
- 2 oranges, peeled and segmented
- 1/2 cup walnuts, chopped
- Olive oil for drizzling
- Salt and pepper to taste

Instructions:

1. In a large bowl, combine baby spinach, orange segments, and chopped walnuts.
2. Drizzle with olive oil and toss gently to coat.
3. Season with salt and pepper to taste.
4. Serve immediately and savor this nutritious Spinach and Orange Salad!

Nutritional Information (per serving):
Cal: 270 | Carbs: 30g | Pro: 7g | Fat: 16g
Sugars: 17g | Fiber: 7g

15. Grilled Zucchini and Tomato Salad

Preparation time: 15 minutes
Servings: 2

Ingredients:

- 2 medium zucchini, sliced
- 1 cup cherry tomatoes, halved
- 2 tbsp olive oil
- 1 tsp dried oregano
- Salt and pepper to taste

Instructions:

1. Preheat a grill pan or outdoor grill over medium heat.
2. In a bowl, toss zucchini slices and cherry tomatoes with olive oil, dried oregano, salt, and pepper.
3. Grill the zucchini and tomatoes for 2-3 minutes per side until they have grill marks and are tender.
4. Transfer to a serving plate and enjoy this Grilled Zucchini and Tomato Salad!

Nutritional Information (per serving):
Cal: 160 | Carbs: 12g | Pro: 3g | Fat: 12g
Sugars: 8g | Fiber: 3g

16. Tuna Salad with Avocado & Chickpeas

Preparation time: 10 minutes
Servings: 2

Ingredients:

- 1 can (5 oz) tuna, drained
- 1 avocado, diced
- 1 cup canned chickpeas, drained and rinsed
- 1/4 red onion, finely chopped
- Lemon juice for drizzling

Instructions:

1. In a bowl, combine drained tuna, diced avocado, chickpeas, and finely chopped red onion.
2. Drizzle with fresh lemon juice.
3. Toss gently to mix.
4. Serve immediately and enjoy this protein-packed Tuna Salad with Avocado and Chickpeas!

Nutritional Information (per serving):
Cal: 380 | Carbs: 26g | Pro: 22g | Fat: 24g
Sugars: 5g | Fiber: 12g

17. Roasted Sweet Potato & Kale Salad

Preparation time: 20 minutes
Servings: 2

Ingredients:

- 2 medium sweet potatoes, peeled and cubed
- 2 cups kale, chopped
- 2 tbsp olive oil
- 1 tsp smoked paprika
- Salt and pepper to taste

Instructions:

1. Preheat the oven to 400°F (200°C).
2. Toss sweet potato cubes with olive oil, smoked paprika, salt, and pepper.
3. Roast in the oven for 15-20 minutes or until sweet potatoes are tender.
4. In a bowl, combine roasted sweet potatoes with chopped kale.
5. Serve warm and enjoy this Roasted Sweet Potato and Kale Salad!

Nutritional Information (per serving):
Cal: 280 | Carbs: 41g | Pro: 4g | Fat: 12g
Sugars: 7g | Fiber: 6g

18. Asian-Inspired Quinoa Salad

Preparation time: 15 minutes
Servings: 2

Ingredients:

- 1 cup cooked quinoa, cooled
- 1 cup shredded cabbage
- 1 carrot, julienned
- 2 green onions, sliced
- Soy ginger dressing (store-bought or homemade)

Instructions:

1. In a bowl, combine cooked quinoa, shredded cabbage, julienned carrot, and sliced green onions.
2. Toss with your favorite soy ginger dressing.
3. Serve chilled and enjoy this flavorful Asian-Inspired Quinoa Salad!

Nutritional Information (per serving):
Cal: 250 | Carbs: 43g | Pro: 8g | Fat: 5g
Sugars: 5g | Fiber: 6g

19. Warm Brussels Sprout Salad

Preparation time: 15 minutes
Servings: 2

Ingredients:

- 2 cups Brussels sprouts, halved
- 1/2 cup pecans, chopped
- 2 tbsp olive oil
- 1 tbsp balsamic vinegar
- Salt and pepper to taste

Instructions:

1. In a skillet, heat olive oil over medium heat.
2. Add Brussels sprouts and sauté until they are golden brown and tender.
3. Drizzle with balsamic vinegar, add chopped pecans, and toss.
4. Season with salt and pepper to taste.
5. Serve warm and savor this delightful Warm Brussels Sprout Salad with Pecans!

Nutritional Information (per serving):
Cal: 280 | Carbs: 15g | Pro: 7g | Fat: 24g
Sugars: 3g | Fiber: 7g

20. Avocado, Grapefruit, & Shrimp Salad

Preparation time: 15 minutes
Servings: 2

Ingredients:

- 12 large shrimp, cooked and peeled
- 1 avocado, diced
- 1 pink grapefruit, segmented
- Mixed salad greens
- Citrus vinaigrette dressing (store-bought or homemade)

Instructions:

1. In a bowl, combine cooked shrimp, diced avocado, and segmented grapefruit.
2. Arrange mixed salad greens on serving plates.
3. Top the greens with the shrimp, avocado, and grapefruit mixture.
4. Drizzle with citrus vinaigrette dressing.
5. Serve immediately and enjoy this refreshing Avocado, Grapefruit, and Shrimp Salad!

Nutritional Information (per serving):
Cal: 320 | Carbs: 24g | Pro: 21g | Fat: 18g
Sugars: 9g | Fiber: 9g

Fish and Seafood

1. Baked Salmon with Lemon and Dill

Preparation time: 10 minutes
Servings: 2

Ingredients:

- 2 salmon fillets
- 1 lemon, sliced
- Fresh dill, chopped
- Salt and pepper to taste
- Olive oil for drizzling

Instructions:

1. Preheat the oven to 400°F (200°C).
2. Place the salmon fillets on a baking sheet lined with parchment paper.
3. Season the salmon with salt and pepper.
4. Lay lemon slices on top of each fillet and sprinkle fresh dill over them.
5. Drizzle a bit of olive oil over each fillet.
6. Bake in the preheated oven for 12-15 minutes or until the salmon flakes easily with a fork.
7. Serve with additional lemon wedges and a sprinkle of fresh dill.

Nutritional Information (per serving):
Cal: 350 | Carbs: 1g | Pro: 45g | Fat: 18g
Sugars: 0g | Fiber: 0g

2. Garlic & Herb Grilled Shrimp Skewers

Preparation time: 15 minutes
Servings: 2

Ingredients:

- 1 pound large shrimp, peeled and deveined
- 2 tablespoons olive oil
- 3 cloves garlic, minced
- Fresh herbs (rosemary, thyme, or oregano), chopped
- Salt and pepper to taste

Instructions:

1. In a bowl, mix shrimp with olive oil, minced garlic, chopped herbs, salt, and pepper.
2. Preheat the grill to medium-high heat.
3. Thread the shrimp onto skewers.
4. Grill for 2-3 minutes per side or until the shrimp are opaque and lightly charred.
5. Remove from the grill and serve immediately.

Nutritional Information (per serving):
Cal: 230 | Carbs: 2g | Pro: 24g | Fat: 14g
Sugars: 0g | Fiber: 0g

3. Seared Tuna with Sesame Ginger Sauce

Preparation time: 10 minutes
Servings: 2

Ingredients:

- 2 tuna steaks
- 2 tablespoons soy sauce (low-sodium)
- 1 tablespoon sesame oil
- 1 tablespoon fresh ginger, grated
- 1 tablespoon sesame seeds

Instructions:

1. Pat the tuna steaks dry and season with salt and pepper.
2. In a bowl, mix soy sauce, sesame oil, and grated ginger.
3. Heat a non-stick skillet over medium-high heat.
4. Sear the tuna steaks for 1-2 minutes per side, or until the desired doneness.
5. Pour the sesame ginger sauce over the seared tuna and sprinkle with sesame seeds.
6. Serve immediately.

Nutritional Information (per serving):
Cal: 280 | Carbs: 2g | Pro: 40g | Fat: 12g
Sugars: 0g | Fiber: 0g

4. Lemon Herb Baked Cod

Preparation time: 10 minutes
Servings: 2

Ingredients:

- 2 cod fillets
- 1 lemon, juiced
- Fresh parsley, chopped
- 2 tablespoons olive oil
- Salt and pepper to taste

Instructions:

1. Preheat the oven to 375°F (190°C).
2. Place the cod fillets in a baking dish.
3. In a small bowl, mix lemon juice, chopped parsley, olive oil, salt, and pepper.

4. Pour the lemon herb mixture over the cod fillets.
5. Bake for 15-20 minutes or until the cod flakes easily with a fork.
6. Serve with additional lemon wedges if desired.

Nutritional Information (per serving):
Cal: 250 | Carbs: 2g | Pro: 30g | Fat: 14g
Sugars: 0g | Fiber: 0g

5. Spicy Grilled Salmon

Preparation time: 15 minutes
Servings: 2

Ingredients:

- 2 salmon fillets
- 1 teaspoon chili powder
- 1/2 teaspoon cumin
- Salt and pepper to taste
- Avocado Salsa: 1 avocado, diced; 1 tomato, diced; 1/4 cup red onion, finely chopped; Fresh cilantro, chopped; Lime juice

Instructions:

1. Preheat the grill to medium-high heat.
2. In a small bowl, mix chili powder, cumin, salt, and pepper.
3. Rub the spice mixture onto the salmon fillets.
4. Grill the salmon for 3-4 minutes per side or until cooked through.
5. In a separate bowl, combine diced avocado, tomato, red onion, cilantro, and lime juice to make the salsa.
6. Top the grilled salmon with the avocado salsa before serving.

Nutritional Information (per serving):
Cal: 380 | Carbs: 9g | Pro: 30g | Fat: 26g
Sugars: 2g | Fiber: 5g

6. Herb-Crusted Baked Tilapia

Preparation time: 10 minutes
Servings: 2

Ingredients:

- 2 tilapia fillets
- 2 tablespoons olive oil
- 1/4 cup fresh herbs (parsley, dill, or cilantro), chopped
- 1/4 cup almond flour
- Salt and pepper to taste

Instructions:

1. Preheat the oven to 400°F (200°C).
2. Place tilapia fillets on a baking sheet lined with parchment paper.
3. In a bowl, mix olive oil, chopped herbs, almond flour, salt, and pepper.
4. Coat each tilapia fillet with the herb mixture.
5. Bake for 12-15 minutes or until the tilapia is cooked through and the crust is golden.
6. Serve immediately.

Nutritional Information (per serving):
Cal: 270 | Carbs: 2g | Pro: 30g | Fat: 16g
Sugars: 0g | Fiber: 1g

7. Teriyaki Glazed Salmon

Preparation time: 10 minutes
Servings: 2

Ingredients:

- 2 salmon fillets
- 2 tablespoons low-sodium soy sauce
- 1 tablespoon honey
- 1 teaspoon fresh ginger, grated
- 1 clove garlic, minced

Instructions:

1. Preheat the oven to 400°F (200°C).
2. In a small bowl, mix soy sauce, honey, grated ginger, and minced garlic to make the teriyaki glaze.
3. Place the salmon fillets on a baking sheet lined with parchment paper.
4. Brush the teriyaki glaze over each salmon fillet.
5. Bake for 12-15 minutes or until the salmon flakes easily with a fork.
6. Serve with steamed vegetables or your choice of side.

Nutritional Information (per serving):
Cal: 320 | Carbs: 8g | Pro: 35g | Fat: 16g
Sugars: 7g | Fiber: 0g

8. Coconut-Curry Shrimp Stir-Fry

Preparation time: 15 minutes
Servings: 2

Ingredients:

- 1 pound large shrimp, peeled and deveined
- 1 cup broccoli florets
- 1 bell pepper, sliced
- 2 tablespoons coconut milk
- 2 tablespoons curry powder
- Salt and pepper to taste

Instructions:

1. In a wok or large skillet, sauté shrimp, broccoli, bell pepper until shrimp turns pink.
2. In a small bowl, mix coconut milk and curry powder.
3. Pour the coconut-curry mixture over the shrimp and vegetables.
4. Stir-fry for an additional 2-3 minutes until everything is well-coated and heated through.
5. Season with salt and pepper to taste.
6. Serve over cauliflower rice or your choice of grains.

Nutritional Information (per serving):
Cal: 280 | Carbs: 12g | Pro: 30g | Fat: 14g
Sugars: 4g | Fiber: 5g

9. Grilled Swordfish with Mango Salsa

Preparation time: 15 minutes
Servings: 2

Ingredients:

- 2 swordfish steaks
- 1 mango, diced
- 1/4 cup red onion, finely chopped
- Fresh cilantro, chopped
- 1 lime, juiced
- Salt and pepper to taste

Instructions:

1. Preheat the grill to medium-high heat.
2. Season swordfish steaks with salt and pepper.
3. Grill the swordfish for 3-4 minutes per side or until it reaches your desired doneness.
4. In a bowl, mix diced mango, red onion, cilantro, and lime juice to make the salsa.
5. Top the grilled swordfish with mango salsa before serving.

Nutritional Information (per serving):
Cal: 320 | Carbs: 14g | Pro: 35g | Fat: 15g
Sugars: 10g | Fiber: 2g

10. Mediterranean Baked Halibut

Preparation time: 10 minutes
Servings: 2

Ingredients:

- 2 halibut fillets
- 2 tablespoons olive oil
- 1 tablespoon lemon juice
- 1 teaspoon dried oregano
- 1 teaspoon dried thyme
- Salt and pepper to taste

Instructions:

1. Preheat the oven to 375°F (190°C).
2. Place the halibut fillets in a baking dish.
3. In a small bowl, mix olive oil, lemon juice, dried oregano, dried thyme, salt, pepper.
4. Drizzle the herb mixture over the halibut fillets.
5. Bake for 15-20 minutes or until the halibut flakes easily with a fork.
6. Serve with a side of sautéed spinach or your favorite greens.

Nutritional Information (per serving):
Cal: 280 | Carbs: 1g | Pro: 30g | Fat: 18g
Sugars: 0g | Fiber: 0g

11. Lemon Garlic Butter Shrimp

Preparation time: 10 minutes
Servings: 2

Ingredients:

- 1 pound large shrimp, peeled and deveined
- 4 tablespoons unsalted butter
- 4 cloves garlic, minced
- 1 lemon, juiced
- Salt and pepper to taste

Instructions:

1. In a large skillet, melt the butter over medium heat.

2. Add minced garlic and sauté for 1-2 minutes until fragrant.
3. Add the shrimp to the skillet, cooking for 2-3 minutes on each side until they turn pink.
4. Squeeze the lemon juice over the shrimp and season with salt and pepper to taste.
5. Stir well to coat the shrimp in the garlic lemon butter sauce.
6. Serve immediately, garnished with fresh parsley if desired.

Nutritional Information (per serving):
Cal: 354 | Carbs: 4g | Pro: 46g | Fat: 18g
Sugars: 0g | Fiber: 0g

12. Pan-Seared Sea Bass

Preparation time: 15 minutes
Servings: 2

Ingredients:

- 2 sea bass fillets
- 1 cup cherry tomatoes, halved
- 2 tablespoons olive oil
- 1/4 cup fresh basil, chopped
- Salt and pepper to taste

Instructions:

1. Season sea bass fillets with salt and pepper on both sides.
2. In a skillet, heat olive oil over medium-high heat.
3. Place sea bass fillets in the skillet, cooking for 3-4 minutes on each side until golden and cooked through.
4. In the last minute of cooking, add cherry tomatoes to the skillet, allowing them to blister.
5. Sprinkle fresh basil over the sea bass and tomatoes.
6. Serve the sea bass fillets over a bed of blistered tomatoes and garnish with extra basil.

Nutritional Information (per serving):
Cal: 321 | Carbs: 3g | Pro: 26g | Fat: 23g
Sugars: 1g | Fiber: 1g

13. Cajun-Spiced Baked Catfish

Preparation time: 10 minutes
Servings: 2

Ingredients:

- 2 catfish fillets
- 2 tablespoons olive oil
- 2 teaspoons Cajun seasoning
- 1 lemon, sliced
- Fresh parsley for garnish

Instructions:

1. Preheat the oven to 400°F (200°C) and line a baking sheet with parchment paper.
2. Place catfish fillets on the prepared baking sheet.
3. Drizzle olive oil over the fillets and rub with Cajun seasoning on both sides.
4. Arrange lemon slices over the catfish.
5. Bake for 15-18 minutes or until the catfish is flaky and cooked through.
6. Garnish with fresh parsley before serving.

Nutritional Information (per serving):
Cal: 284 | Carbs: 2g | Pro: 28g | Fat: 18g
Sugars: 0g | Fiber: 1g

14. Sesame Crusted Ahi Tuna Salad

Preparation time: 15 minutes
Servings: 2

Ingredients:

- 2 ahi tuna steaks
- 2 tablespoons sesame seeds
- 4 cups mixed salad greens
- 1 cucumber, sliced
- Ginger-sesame dressing (store-bought or homemade)

Instructions:

1. Pat the ahi tuna steaks dry and coat them with sesame seeds on both sides.
2. Heat a non-stick skillet over high heat.
3. Sear the tuna steaks for 1-2 minutes on each side for a rare to medium-rare doneness.
4. Slice the tuna into thin strips.
5. In a large bowl, combine salad greens and sliced cucumber.
6. Top the salad with sesame-crusted tuna strips and drizzle with ginger-sesame dressing.

Nutritional Information (per serving):
Cal: 276 | Carbs: 10g | Pro: 36g | Fat: 10g
Sugars: 4g | Fiber: 3g

15. Pesto Grilled Scallop Skewers

Preparation time: 12 minutes
Servings: 2

Ingredients:

- 1 pound scallops, cleaned and patted dry
- 4 tablespoons homemade or store-bought pesto sauce
- 1 lemon, zested and juiced
- Olive oil for brushing
- Wooden skewers, soaked in water for 30 minutes

Instructions:

1. Preheat the grill to medium-high heat.
2. In a bowl, combine scallops with pesto sauce, lemon zest, and lemon juice. Let them marinate for 10 minutes.
3. Thread marinated scallops onto the soaked skewers.
4. Brush the skewers with olive oil to prevent sticking.
5. Grill the skewers for 2-3 minutes on each side until scallops are cooked through and have grill marks.
6. Serve the scallop skewers with additional pesto sauce for dipping.

Nutritional Information (per serving):
Cal: 298 | Carbs: 5g | Pro: 30g | Fat: 18g
Sugars: 1g | Fiber: 1g

16. Miso-Glazed Black Cod

Preparation time: 10 minutes
Servings: 2

Ingredients:

- 2 black cod fillets
- 3 tablespoons white miso paste
- 2 tablespoons mirin (Japanese sweet rice wine)
- 1 tablespoon soy sauce
- 1 tablespoon honey

Instructions:

1. Preheat the oven to 400°F (200°C).
2. In a small bowl, whisk together miso paste, mirin, soy sauce, and honey to make the glaze.
3. Place black cod fillets on a baking sheet lined with parchment paper.
4. Brush the miso glaze over the cod fillets.
5. Bake for 12-15 minutes or until the cod is opaque and flakes easily.
6. Serve the miso-glazed black cod over steamed brown rice or quinoa.

Nutritional Information (per serving):
Cal: 295 | Carbs: 20g | Pro: 30g | Fat: 10g
Sugars: 11g | Fiber: 1g

17. Shrimp and Asparagus Stir-Fry

Preparation time: 15 minutes
Servings: 2

Ingredients:

- 1 pound shrimp, peeled and deveined
- 1 bunch asparagus, trimmed and cut into bite-sized pieces
- 2 tablespoons olive oil
- 3 cloves garlic, minced
- 1 tablespoon low-sodium soy sauce

Instructions:

1. Heat olive oil in a wok or large skillet over medium-high heat.
2. Add minced garlic and stir-fry for 1 minute until fragrant.
3. Add shrimp to the wok, cooking for 2-3 minutes until they start turning pink.
4. Add asparagus to the wok and continue stir-frying for an additional 3-4 minutes until asparagus is tender-crisp.
5. Drizzle soy sauce over the shrimp and asparagus, tossing to coat evenly.
6. Serve the shrimp and asparagus stir-fry over quinoa or brown rice.

Nutritional Information (per serving):
Cal: 268 | Carbs: 8g | Pro: 34g | Fat: 11g
Sugars: 3g | Fiber: 4g

18. Baked Haddock with Vegetables

Preparation time: 15 minutes
Servings: 2

Ingredients:

- 2 haddock fillets
- 2 cups cherry tomatoes, halved
- 1 zucchini, sliced
- 1 red onion, sliced
- 2 tablespoons olive oil
- Italian seasoning, to taste

Instructions:

1. Preheat the oven to 400°F (200°C) and line a baking sheet with parchment paper.
2. Place haddock fillets on the prepared baking sheet.
3. In a bowl, toss cherry tomatoes, zucchini, and red onion with olive oil and Italian seasoning.
4. Spread the vegetable mixture around the haddock fillets.
5. Bake for 15-18 minutes or until the haddock is flaky and the vegetables are roasted.
6. Serve the baked haddock over the roasted vegetables.

Nutritional Information (per serving):
Cal: 292 | Carbs: 12g | Pro: 32g | Fat: 14g
Sugars: 7g | Fiber: 3g

19. Codfish Ceviche with Avocado

Preparation time: 20 minutes (plus chilling time)
Servings: 2

Ingredients:

- 1/2 pound fresh cod fillet, diced
- 1 avocado, diced
- 1/2 red onion, finely chopped
- 1 jalapeño, seeded and minced
- 1/4 cup fresh cilantro, chopped
- Juice of 2 limes
- Salt and pepper to taste

Instructions:

1. In a bowl, combine diced cod, diced avocado, chopped red onion, minced jalapeño, and chopped cilantro.
2. Squeeze the juice of two limes over the mixture and toss gently.
3. Season with salt and pepper to taste, stirring to combine.
4. Cover the bowl and refrigerate for at least 30 minutes to allow the flavors to meld.
5. Serve the codfish ceviche chilled, garnished with additional cilantro.

Nutritional Information (per serving):
Cal: 268 | Carbs: 12g | Pro: 24g | Fat: 16g
Sugars: 1g | Fiber: 7g

20. Grilled Sardines

Preparation time: 15 minutes
Servings: 2

Ingredients:

- 4 fresh sardines, cleaned and gutted
- 2 tablespoons olive oil
- Zest and juice of 1 lemon
- 2 teaspoons fresh thyme, chopped
- Salt and pepper to taste

Instructions:

1. Preheat the grill to medium-high heat.
2. Score the sardines on both sides and rub with olive oil.
3. In a bowl, mix lemon zest, lemon juice, and chopped thyme.
4. Brush the sardines with the lemon and thyme mixture.
5. Season the sardines with salt and pepper to taste.
6. Grill the sardines for 3-4 minutes on each side until they are cooked through.
7. Serve the grilled sardines with additional lemon wedges.

Nutritional Information (per serving):
Cal: 246 | Carbs: 2g | Pro: 28g | Fat: 14g
Sugars: 0g | Fiber: 0g

Poultry

1. Turmeric & Garlic Roasted Chicken

Preparation time: 10 minutes
Servings: 2

Ingredients:

- 2 bone-in, skin-on chicken thighs
- 1 tablespoon olive oil
- 1 teaspoon turmeric powder
- 3 cloves garlic, minced
- Salt and black pepper to taste

Instructions:

1. Preheat the oven to 400°F (200°C).
2. In a small bowl, mix olive oil, turmeric powder, minced garlic, salt, and black pepper to create a paste.
3. Pat the chicken thighs dry with a paper towel and rub the turmeric mixture evenly over each piece.
4. Place the chicken thighs on a baking sheet lined with parchment paper, skin side up.
5. Roast in the preheated oven for 35-40 minutes or until the internal temperature reaches 165°F (74°C).
6. Allow the chicken to rest for a few minutes before serving.

Nutritional Information (per serving):
Cal: 320 | Carbs: 0g | Pro: 23g | Fat: 26g
Sugars: 0g | Fiber: 0g

2. Lemon Herb Grilled Chicken Breasts

Preparation time: 15 minutes (marinating time included)
Servings: 2

Ingredients:

- 2 boneless, skinless chicken breasts
- 2 tablespoons olive oil
- Juice of 1 lemon
- 1 teaspoon dried mixed herbs (thyme, rosemary, oregano)
- Salt and black pepper to taste

Instructions:

1. In a bowl, whisk together olive oil, lemon juice, dried herbs, salt, and black pepper.
2. Place the chicken breasts in a resealable plastic bag and pour the marinade over them. Seal the bag and let it marinate in the refrigerator for at least 30 minutes.
3. Preheat the grill or grill pan over medium-high heat.
4. Grill the chicken breasts for 6-7 minutes per side or until the internal temperature reaches 165°F (74°C).
5. Allow the chicken to rest for a few minutes before slicing and serving.

Nutritional Information (per serving):
Cal: 280 | Carbs: 2g | Pro: 25g | Fat: 18g
Sugars: 0g | Fiber: 0g

3. Cumin & Paprika Turkey Burgers

Preparation time: 15 minutes
Servings: 2

Ingredients:

- 1/2 lb ground turkey
- 1 teaspoon ground cumin
- 1 teaspoon smoked paprika
- Salt and black pepper to taste
- Olive oil (for cooking)

Instructions:

1. In a bowl, mix ground turkey, cumin, smoked paprika, salt, and black pepper until well combined.
2. Divide the mixture into two portions and shape them into burger patties.
3. Heat olive oil in a skillet over medium-high heat.
4. Cook the turkey burgers for 4-5 minutes per side or until they reach an internal temperature of 165°F (74°C).
5. Serve the turkey burgers with your favorite anti-inflammatory side dishes.

Nutritional Information (per serving):
Cal: 220 | Carbs: 0g | Pro: 25g | Fat: 13g
Sugars: 0g | Fiber: 0g

4. Baked Rosemary Chicken Thighs

Preparation time: 10 minutes
Servings: 2

Ingredients:

- 2 bone-in, skin-on chicken thighs
- 1 tablespoon olive oil
- 1 teaspoon dried rosemary
- Salt and black pepper to taste

Instructions:

1. Preheat the oven to 400°F (200°C).
2. Rub chicken thighs with olive oil and season with dried rosemary, salt, and black pepper.
3. Place the chicken thighs on a baking sheet lined with parchment paper.
4. Bake for 35-40 minutes or until the internal temperature reaches 165°F (74°C).
5. Allow the chicken to rest for a few minutes before serving.

Nutritional Information (per serving):
Cal: 300 | Carbs: 0g | Pro: 23g | Fat: 22g
Sugars: 0g | Fiber: 0g

5. Greek Yogurt Marinated Chicken

Preparation time: 20 minutes (marinating time included)
Servings: 2

Ingredients:

- 2 boneless, skinless chicken breasts, cut into cubes
- 1/2 cup plain Greek yogurt
- 1 tablespoon lemon juice
- 1 teaspoon dried oregano
- Salt and black pepper to taste

Instructions:

1. In a bowl, mix Greek yogurt, lemon juice, dried oregano, salt, and black pepper.
2. Add the chicken cubes to the yogurt mixture, ensuring they are well-coated. Marinate in the refrigerator for at least 1 hour.
3. Preheat the grill or grill pan over medium-high heat.
4. Thread the marinated chicken cubes onto skewers.
5. Grill the chicken skewers for 5-6 minutes per side or until fully cooked.
6. Serve the skewers with a side of anti-inflammatory vegetables or a Greek salad.

Nutritional Information (per serving):
Cal: 220 | Carbs: 3g | Pro: 30g | Fat: 9g
Sugars: 2g | Fiber: 0g

6. Basil & Lemon Roasted Turkey Breast

Preparation time: 15 minutes
Servings: 2

Ingredients:

- 1/2 lb turkey breast, boneless and skinless
- 2 tablespoons olive oil
- Handful of fresh basil leaves, chopped
- Zest of 1 lemon
- Salt and black pepper to taste

Instructions:

1. Preheat the oven to 375°F (190°C).
2. In a small bowl, mix olive oil, chopped basil, lemon zest, salt, and black pepper.
3. Place the turkey breast in a baking dish and rub the basil-lemon mixture over it.
4. Roast in the preheated oven for 25-30 minutes or until the internal temperature reaches 165°F (74°C).
5. Allow the turkey breast to rest for a few minutes before slicing and serving.

Nutritional Information (per serving):
Cal: 180 | Carbs: 1g | Pro: 30g | Fat: 6g
Sugars: 0g | Fiber: 0g

7. Coconut-Curry Chicken Stir-Fry

Preparation time: 20 minutes
Servings: 2

Ingredients:

- 1 lb boneless, skinless chicken breast, thinly sliced
- 2 tablespoons coconut oil
- 2 teaspoons yellow curry powder
- 1 cup broccoli florets
- Salt and black pepper to taste

Instructions:

1. In a large skillet or wok, heat coconut oil over medium-high heat.
2. Add sliced chicken to the pan and cook until browned.
3. Sprinkle curry powder over the chicken and toss to coat evenly.
4. Add broccoli florets to the pan and continue to stir-fry until the chicken is fully cooked and the broccoli is tender-crisp.

5. Season with salt and black pepper to taste.
6. Serve the coconut-curry chicken stir-fry over a bed of quinoa or brown rice.

Nutritional Information (per serving):
Cal: 320 | Carbs: 5g | Pro: 35g | Fat: 18g
Sugars: 1g | Fiber: 2g

8. Garlic & Herb Grilled Turkey

Preparation time: 15 minutes (marinating time included)
Servings: 2

Ingredients:

- 1 lb turkey tenderloin
- 2 tablespoons olive oil
- 3 cloves garlic, minced
- 1 teaspoon dried mixed herbs (thyme, rosemary, oregano)
- Salt and black pepper to taste

Instructions:

1. In a small bowl, mix olive oil, minced garlic, dried herbs, salt, and black pepper.
2. Rub the mixture over the turkey tenderloin and let it marinate for at least 30 minutes.
3. Preheat the grill or grill pan over medium-high heat.
4. Grill the turkey tenderloin for 15-20 minutes, turning occasionally, until fully cooked with an internal temperature of 165°F (74°C).
5. Allow the turkey to rest for a few minutes before slicing and serving.

Nutritional Information (per serving):
Cal: 280 | Carbs: 0g | Pro: 30g | Fat: 17g
Sugars: 0g | Fiber: 0g

9. Almond-Crusted Chicken Tenders

Preparation time: 20 minutes
Servings: 2

Ingredients:

- 1 lb chicken tenders
- 1/2 cup almond flour
- 1 teaspoon paprika
- Salt and black pepper to taste
- Olive oil (for cooking)

Instructions:

1. In a shallow bowl, mix almond flour, paprika, salt, and black pepper.
2. Coat each chicken tender in the almond flour mixture, pressing it onto the chicken.
3. Heat olive oil in a skillet over medium heat.
4. Cook the almond-crusted chicken tenders for 4-5 minutes per side or until golden brown and fully cooked.
5. Serve with a side of anti-inflammatory vegetables or a light salad.

Nutritional Information (per serving):
Cal: 320 | Carbs: 3g | Pro: 30g | Fat: 21g
Sugars: 1g | Fiber: 2g

10. Spinach & Feta Stuffed Chicken Breast

Preparation time: 20 minutes
Servings: 2

Ingredients:

- 2 boneless, skinless chicken breasts
- 1 cup fresh spinach, chopped
- 1/2 cup feta cheese, crumbled
- 1 teaspoon dried oregano
- Salt and black pepper to taste

Instructions:

1. Preheat the oven to 375°F (190°C).
2. In a bowl, mix chopped spinach, crumbled feta, dried oregano, salt, and black pepper.
3. Slice each chicken breast horizontally to create a pocket without cutting through.
4. Stuff each chicken breast with the spinach and feta mixture.
5. Season the outside of the chicken breasts with salt and black pepper.
6. Place the stuffed chicken breasts in a baking dish and bake for 25-30 minutes or until fully cooked.
7. Allow the stuffed chicken breasts to rest for a few minutes before serving.

Nutritional Information (per serving):
Cal: 280 | Carbs: 2g | Pro: 35g | Fat: 14g
Sugars: 1g | Fiber: 1g

11. Paprika and Thyme Roasted Quail

Preparation time: 10 minutes

Servings: 2

Ingredients:

- 2 quails
- 1 teaspoon paprika
- 1 teaspoon dried thyme
- Salt and pepper to taste
- 1 tablespoon olive oil

Instructions:

1. Preheat your oven to 400°F (200°C).
2. Rinse the quails and pat them dry with paper towels.
3. In a small bowl, mix paprika, dried thyme, salt, and pepper.
4. Rub the quails with olive oil, ensuring they are well-coated.
5. Sprinkle the paprika and thyme mixture evenly over the quails, rubbing it into the skin.
6. Place the quails on a baking sheet or in an oven-safe dish.
7. Roast in the preheated oven for 25-30 minutes or until the internal temperature reaches 165°F (74°C).
8. Remove from the oven, let them rest for a few minutes, and serve.

Nutritional Information (per serving):
Cal: 320 | Carbs: 0g | Pro: 26g | Fat: 22g
Sugars: 0g | Fiber: 0g

12. Orange Glazed Grilled Chicken

Preparation time: 15 minutes (plus marinating time)
Servings: 2

Ingredients:

- 4 chicken drumsticks
- 1 orange (juiced and zested)
- 2 tablespoons soy sauce (low-sodium)
- 1 tablespoon honey
- 1 teaspoon grated ginger

Instructions:

1. In a bowl, whisk together orange juice, orange zest, soy sauce, honey, and grated ginger to make the marinade.
2. Place chicken drumsticks in a resealable plastic bag or a shallow dish and pour half of the marinade over them.
3. Marinate in the refrigerator for at least 30 minutes (or overnight for more flavor).
4. Preheat the grill to medium-high heat.
5. Grill the drumsticks for 15-20 minutes, turning occasionally, until fully cooked.
6. Brush the remaining marinade over the drumsticks during the last few minutes of grilling.
7. Remove from the grill, let them rest for a couple of minutes, and serve.

Nutritional Information (per serving):
Cal: 220 | Carbs: 15g | Pro: 20g | Fat: 10g
Sugars: 12g | Fiber: 1g

13. Balsamic Glazed Chicken

Preparation time: 10 minutes
Servings: 2

Ingredients:

- 2 boneless, skinless chicken breasts
- 1 cup Brussels sprouts, halved
- 2 tablespoons balsamic vinegar
- 1 tablespoon olive oil
- Salt and pepper to taste

Instructions:

1. Preheat the oven to 400°F (200°C).
2. Season chicken breasts and Brussels sprouts with salt and pepper.
3. In a bowl, mix balsamic vinegar and olive oil.
4. Place chicken breasts and Brussels sprouts on a baking sheet.
5. Brush the balsamic mixture over the chicken and Brussels sprouts.
6. Roast for 20-25 minutes or until the chicken is cooked through and Brussels sprouts are tender.
7. Remove from the oven, let it rest for a few minutes, and serve.

Nutritional Information (per serving):
Cal: 280 | Carbs: 12g | Pro: 30g | Fat: 12g
Sugars: 4g | Fiber: 4g

14. Honey Mustard Roasted Chicken Wings

Preparation time: 10 minutes
Servings: 2

Ingredients:

- 8 chicken wings
- 2 tablespoons Dijon mustard
- 1 tablespoon honey
- 1 tablespoon olive oil
- Salt and pepper to taste

Instructions:

1. Preheat the oven to 400°F (200°C).
2. In a bowl, mix Dijon mustard, honey, olive oil, salt, and pepper.
3. Coat the chicken wings with the honey mustard mixture.
4. Place wings on a baking sheet lined with parchment paper.
5. Roast for 25-30 minutes or until wings are golden and cooked through.
6. Remove from the oven, let them rest for a few minutes, and serve.

Nutritional Information (per serving):
Cal: 330 | Carbs: 6g | Pro: 24g | Fat: 24g
Sugars: 5g | Fiber: 0g

15. Mediterranean Turkey Meatballs

Preparation time: 15 minutes
Servings: 2

Ingredients:

- 1/2 lb ground turkey
- 1/4 cup breadcrumbs
- 1 teaspoon dried oregano
- 1/2 teaspoon garlic powder
- Salt and pepper to taste
- Tzatziki sauce for serving

Instructions:

1. Preheat the oven to 400°F (200°C).
2. In a bowl, combine ground turkey, breadcrumbs, dried oregano, garlic powder, salt, and pepper.
3. Form the mixture into small meatballs and place them on a baking sheet.
4. Bake for 15-20 minutes or until the meatballs are cooked through.
5. Serve the meatballs with tzatziki sauce.

Nutritional Information (per serving):
Cal: 230 | Carbs: 8g | Pro: 27g | Fat: 10g
Sugars: 1g | Fiber: 1g

16. Lemon Garlic Chicken Skillet

Preparation time: 10 minutes
Servings: 2

Ingredients:

- 2 boneless, skinless chicken breasts
- 2 tablespoons olive oil
- 4 cloves garlic, minced
- 1 lemon (juiced and zested)
- Salt and pepper to taste

Instructions:

1. Season chicken breasts with salt and pepper.
2. In a skillet, heat olive oil over medium-high heat.
3. Add chicken breasts and cook for 5-6 minutes on each side or until fully cooked.
4. In the last minute of cooking, add minced garlic to the skillet.
5. Pour lemon juice and zest over the chicken.
6. Cook for an additional minute, allowing the flavors to meld.
7. Remove from the skillet, let it rest for a couple of minutes, and serve.

Nutritional Information (per serving):
Cal: 320 | Carbs: 2g | Pro: 30g | Fat: 22g
Sugars: 0g | Fiber: 0g

17. Pesto Chicken & Vegetable Kebabs

Preparation time: 15 minutes (plus marinating time)
Servings: 2

Ingredients:

- 2 boneless, skinless chicken breasts, cut into chunks
- 1 zucchini, sliced
- 1 red bell pepper, cut into chunks
- 2 tablespoons pesto sauce
- Salt and pepper to taste

Instructions:

1. In a bowl, mix chicken chunks with pesto sauce, salt, and pepper. Marinate for at least 30 minutes.
2. Preheat the grill to medium-high heat.
3. Thread marinated chicken, zucchini, and bell

pepper onto skewers.
4. Grill kebabs for 10-12 minutes, turning occasionally, until the chicken is fully cooked.
5. Remove from the grill, let them rest for a couple of minutes, and serve.

Nutritional Information (per serving):
Cal: 280 | Carbs: 8g | Pro: 30g | Fat: 14g
Sugars: 4g | Fiber: 2g

18. Turmeric & Ginger Chicken Soup

Preparation time: 15 minutes
Servings: 2

Ingredients:

- 2 boneless, skinless chicken thighs
- 1 teaspoon turmeric powder
- 1 teaspoon fresh ginger, grated
- 4 cups low-sodium chicken broth
- Salt and pepper to taste

Instructions:

1. In a pot, bring chicken broth to a simmer.
2. Add chicken thighs, turmeric powder, grated ginger, salt, and pepper.
3. Simmer for 15-20 minutes or until chicken is fully cooked.
4. Remove chicken, shred it, and return it to the pot.
5. Adjust seasoning if necessary and serve.

Nutritional Information (per serving):
Cal: 180 | Carbs: 2g | Pro: 20g | Fat: 10g
Sugars: 0g | Fiber: 0g

19. Rosemary & Dijon Mustard Chicken

Preparation time: 10 minutes
Servings: 2

Ingredients:

- 2 bone-in, skin-on chicken thighs
- 1 tablespoon Dijon mustard
- 1 tablespoon fresh rosemary, chopped
- 1 tablespoon olive oil
- Salt and pepper to taste

Instructions:

1. Preheat the oven to 400°F (200°C).
2. In a bowl, mix Dijon mustard, chopped rosemary, olive oil, salt, and pepper.
3. Coat chicken thighs with the mustard mixture.
4. Place the chicken on a baking sheet.
5. Bake for 30-35 minutes or until the chicken is golden and cooked through.
6. Remove from the oven, let it rest for a couple of minutes, and serve.

Nutritional Information (per serving):
Cal: 300 | Carbs: 1g | Pro: 22g | Fat: 24g
Sugars: 0g | Fiber: 0g

20. Chicken & Vegetable Lettuce Wraps

Preparation time: 15 minutes (plus marinating time)
Servings: 2

Ingredients:

- 2 boneless, skinless chicken breasts
- 1 cup mixed bell peppers, thinly sliced
- 1 cup cucumber, julienned
- 2 tablespoons low-sodium soy sauce
- 1 tablespoon rice vinegar
- Butter lettuce leaves for wrapping

Instructions:

1. In a bowl, mix soy sauce and rice vinegar.
2. Marinate chicken breasts in the mixture for at least 30 minutes.
3. Preheat the grill to medium-high heat.
4. Grill chicken breasts for 6-7 minutes per side or until fully cooked.
5. Let the chicken rest for a couple of minutes before slicing.
6. Assemble lettuce wraps with sliced grilled chicken, mixed bell peppers, and julienned cucumber.
7. Serve immediately.

Nutritional Information (per serving):
Cal: 240 | Carbs: 10g | Pro: 30g | Fat: 8g
Sugars: 5g | Fiber: 2g

Side Dishes

1. Garlic Roasted Brussels Sprouts

Preparation time: 10 minutes
Servings: 2

Ingredients:

- 2 cups Brussels sprouts, halved
- 2 tablespoons olive oil
- 4 cloves garlic, minced
- Salt and black pepper to taste
- Fresh parsley for garnish (optional)

Instructions:

1. Preheat the oven to 400°F (200°C).
2. In a mixing bowl, combine Brussels sprouts, olive oil, minced garlic, salt, black pepper. Toss until Brussels sprouts are evenly coated.
3. Spread the Brussels sprouts in a single layer on a baking sheet.
4. Roast in the preheated oven for 20-25 minutes or until the edges are golden brown and crispy, stirring halfway through.
5. Remove from the oven and garnish with fresh parsley if desired.
6. Serve immediately and enjoy your flavorful and anti-inflammatory side dish!

Nutritional Information (per serving):
Cal: 130 | Carbs: 12g | Pro: 4g | Fat: 8g
Sugars: 2g | Fiber: 4g

2. Lemon Herb Quinoa Pilaf

Preparation time: 15 minutes
Servings: 2

Ingredients:

- 1 cup quinoa, rinsed
- 2 cups vegetable broth
- 1 tablespoon olive oil
- Zest of 1 lemon
- Fresh herbs (such as parsley or cilantro), chopped
- Salt and black pepper to taste

Instructions:

1. In a medium saucepan, combine quinoa and vegetable broth. Bring to a boil, then reduce heat, cover, and simmer for 12-15 minutes or until quinoa is cooked and liquid is absorbed.
2. Fluff the quinoa with a fork and transfer to a mixing bowl.
3. In a small bowl, whisk together olive oil, lemon zest, fresh herbs, salt, black pepper.
4. Pour the dressing over the quinoa and toss to combine.
5. Serve the lemon herb quinoa pilaf as a flavorful and anti-inflammatory side dish.

Nutritional Information (per serving):
Cal: 280 | Carbs: 44g | Pro: 8g | Fat: 9g
Sugars: 1g | Fiber: 5g

3. Turmeric & Cumin Roasted Carrots

Preparation time: 10 minutes
Servings: 2

Ingredients:

- 2 cups baby carrots, washed and trimmed
- 2 tablespoons olive oil
- 1 teaspoon ground turmeric
- 1 teaspoon ground cumin
- Salt and black pepper to taste
- Fresh cilantro for garnish (optional)

Instructions:

1. Preheat the oven to 400°F (200°C).
2. In a bowl, toss baby carrots with olive oil, ground turmeric, ground cumin, salt, and black pepper until well-coated.
3. Spread the carrots in a single layer on a baking sheet.
4. Roast in the preheated oven for 20-25 minutes or until the carrots are tender and slightly caramelized.
5. Garnish with fresh cilantro if desired.
6. Serve as a vibrant and anti-inflammatory side dish.

Nutritional Information (per serving):
Cal: 140 | Carbs: 14g | Pro: 1g | Fat: 10g
Sugars: 6g | Fiber: 4g

4. Roasted Sweet Potato Wedges

Preparation time: 15 minutes
Servings: 2

Ingredients:

- 2 medium sweet potatoes, cut into wedges
- 2 tablespoons olive oil
- 1 teaspoon smoked paprika
- 1 teaspoon garlic powder
- Salt and black pepper to taste
- Fresh rosemary for garnish (optional)

Instructions:

1. Preheat the oven to 425°F (220°C).
2. In a large bowl, toss sweet potato wedges with olive oil, smoked paprika, garlic powder, salt, and black pepper until evenly coated.
3. Spread the wedges in a single layer on a baking sheet.
4. Roast in the preheated oven for 25-30 minutes or until the sweet potatoes are golden brown and crisp, flipping halfway through.
5. Garnish with fresh rosemary if desired.
6. Enjoy these flavorful and anti-inflammatory roasted sweet potato wedges!

Nutritional Information (per serving):
Cal: 180 | Carbs: 26g | Pro: 2g | Fat: 8g
Sugars: 7g | Fiber: 4g

5. Grilled Asparagus with Lemon Zest

Preparation time: 10 minutes
Servings: 2

Ingredients:

- 1 bunch asparagus, tough ends trimmed
- 1 tablespoon olive oil
- Zest of 1 lemon
- Salt and black pepper to taste
- Lemon wedges for serving

Instructions:

1. Preheat a grill or grill pan over medium-high heat.
2. In a bowl, toss asparagus with olive oil, lemon zest, salt, and black pepper.
3. Grill the asparagus for 4-6 minutes, turning occasionally, until they are tender and slightly charred.
4. Transfer to a serving platter, squeeze fresh lemon juice over the top.
5. Serve these grilled asparagus as a delightful and anti-inflammatory side dish.

Nutritional Information (per serving):
Cal: 50 | Carbs: 4g | Pro: 2g | Fat: 4g
Sugars: 2g | Fiber: 2g

6. Sauteed Kale with Garlic & Pine Nuts

Preparation time: 10 minutes
Servings: 2

Ingredients:

- 1 bunch kale, stems removed and leaves chopped
- 2 tablespoons olive oil
- 3 cloves garlic, minced
- 2 tablespoons pine nuts
- Salt and black pepper to taste
- Lemon wedges for serving

Instructions:

1. In a large pan, heat olive oil over medium heat.
2. Add minced garlic and pine nuts, sauté for 1-2 minutes until garlic is fragrant and pine nuts are lightly toasted.
3. Add chopped kale to the pan and sauté for 4-5 minutes until wilted but still vibrant.
4. Season with salt and black pepper to taste.
5. Squeeze fresh lemon juice over the top before serving.
6. Enjoy this quick and anti-inflammatory sautéed kale side dish.

Nutritional Information (per serving):
Cal: 160 | Carbs: 8g | Pro: 4g | Fat: 14g
Sugars: 1g | Fiber: 2g

7. Cauliflower Rice with Herbs

Preparation time: 10 minutes
Servings: 2

Ingredients:

- 1 small head cauliflower, florets only
- 2 tablespoons olive oil
- 1 teaspoon dried herbs (such as thyme or rosemary)
- Salt and black pepper to taste
- Fresh parsley for garnish (optional)

Instructions:

1. Place cauliflower florets in a food processor and pulse until they resemble rice-sized

pieces.
2. In a large pan, heat olive oil over medium heat.
3. Add the cauliflower rice and sauté for 5-7 minutes until tender.
4. Stir in dried herbs and season with salt and black pepper to taste.
5. Garnish with fresh parsley if desired.
6. Serve this cauliflower rice as a delicious and anti-inflammatory grain-free alternative.

Nutritional Information (per serving):
Cal: 100 | Carbs: 8g | Pro: 4g | Fat: 7g
Sugars: 3g | Fiber: 4g

8. Balsamic Glazed Roasted Beets

Preparation time: 15 minutes
Servings: 2

Ingredients:

- 2 medium beets, peeled and sliced
- 2 tablespoons balsamic vinegar
- 1 tablespoon olive oil
- 1 teaspoon honey (optional)
- Salt and black pepper to taste
- Fresh thyme for garnish (optional)

Instructions:

1. Preheat the oven to 400°F (200°C).
2. In a bowl, toss sliced beets with balsamic vinegar, olive oil, honey (if using), salt, and black pepper.
3. Spread the beets in a single layer on a baking sheet.
4. Roast in the preheated oven for 20-25 minutes or until the beets are tender.
5. Garnish with fresh thyme if desired.
6. Serve these balsamic glazed roasted beets as a flavorful and anti-inflammatory side dish.

Nutritional Information (per serving):
Cal: 90 | Carbs: 12g | Pro: 2g | Fat: 4g
Sugars: 9g | Fiber: 3g

9. Ginger Sesame Broccoli Stir-Fry

Preparation time: 15 minutes
Servings: 2

Ingredients:

- 2 cups broccoli florets
- 1 tablespoon sesame oil
- 1 tablespoon low-sodium soy sauce or tamari
- 1 teaspoon fresh ginger, grated
- 1 tablespoon sesame seeds
- Red pepper flakes for heat (optional)

Instructions:

1. Heat sesame oil in a wok or large pan over medium-high heat.
2. Add broccoli florets and stir-fry for 3-4 minutes until they are crisp-tender.
3. In a small bowl, mix soy sauce and grated ginger. Pour over the broccoli and toss to coat evenly.
4. Sprinkle sesame seeds over the top and toss again.
5. Optionally, add red pepper flakes for some heat.
6. Serve this ginger sesame broccoli stir-fry as a quick and anti-inflammatory side dish.

Nutritional Information (per serving):
Cal: 80 | Carbs: 8g | Pro: 3g | Fat: 5g
Sugars: 2g | Fiber: 3g

10. Mediterranean Zucchini Noodles

Preparation time: 10 minutes
Servings: 2

Ingredients:

- 2 medium zucchinis, spiralized
- 2 tablespoons olive oil
- 2 cloves garlic, minced
- 1 cup cherry tomatoes, halved
- 1/4 cup Kalamata olives, sliced
- Fresh basil for garnish

Instructions:

1. In a large pan, heat olive oil over medium heat.
2. Add minced garlic and sauté for 1-2 minutes until fragrant.
3. Add zucchini noodles to the pan and cook for 2-3 minutes until they are just tender.
4. Stir in cherry tomatoes and Kalamata olives, tossing to combine.
5. Cook for an additional 1-2 minutes until tomatoes are slightly softened.
6. Garnish with fresh basil and serve these Mediterranean zucchini noodles as a light

and anti-inflammatory side.

Nutritional Information (per serving):
Cal: 140 | Carbs: 10g | Pro: 3g | Fat: 11g
Sugars: 5g | Fiber: 3g

11. Sweet Potatoes with Coconut Milk

Preparation time: 10 minutes
Servings: 2

Ingredients:

- 2 medium sweet potatoes, peeled and diced
- 1/4 cup coconut milk
- 1 tablespoon coconut oil
- Salt, to taste
- Fresh cilantro, for garnish (optional)

Instructions:

1. Place the diced sweet potatoes in a pot, cover with water, and add a pinch of salt. Boil until the sweet potatoes are fork-tender, about 8-10 minutes.
2. Drain the sweet potatoes and transfer them to a bowl.
3. Mash the sweet potatoes with a fork or potato masher until smooth.
4. Warm the coconut milk and coconut oil together, then add the mixture to the mashed sweet potatoes. Mix well until creamy.
5. Season with salt to taste and garnish with fresh cilantro if desired.

Nutritional Information (per serving):
Cal: 245 | Carbs: 38g | Pro: 3g | Fat: 9g
Sugars: 9g | Fiber: 6g

12. Lemon Dill Cucumber Salad

Preparation time: 5 minutes
Servings: 2

Ingredients:

- 2 cucumbers, thinly sliced
- 1 tablespoon fresh dill, chopped
- Juice of 1 lemon
- 2 tablespoons olive oil
- Salt and pepper, to taste

Instructions:

1. In a bowl, combine the thinly sliced cucumbers and chopped dill.
2. In a small bowl, whisk together lemon juice, olive oil, salt, and pepper.
3. Pour the dressing over the cucumber and dill mixture, tossing to coat evenly.
4. Let the salad marinate for a few minutes before serving.

Nutritional Information (per serving):
Cal: 120 | Carbs: 10g | Pro: 1g | Fat: 9g
Sugars: 3g | Fiber: 2g

13. Coconut-Cilantro Lime Rice

Preparation time: 5 minutes
Servings: 2

Ingredients:

- 1 cup cooked brown rice
- 2 tablespoons shredded coconut (unsweetened)
- 1 tablespoon fresh cilantro, chopped
- Juice of 1 lime
- Salt, to taste

Instructions:

1. In a bowl, fluff the cooked brown rice with a fork.
2. Add shredded coconut and chopped cilantro to the rice.
3. Squeeze the juice of one lime over the mixture.
4. Gently toss the ingredients until well combined.
5. Season with salt to taste.

Nutritional Information (per serving):
Cal: 190 | Carbs: 37g | Pro: 4g | Fat: 4g
Sugars: 1g | Fiber: 3g

14. Roasted Eggplant with Tahini Dressing

Preparation time: 15 minutes
Servings: 2

Ingredients:

- 1 large eggplant, sliced
- 2 tablespoons tahini
- 1 tablespoon olive oil
- 1 clove garlic, minced

- Salt and pepper, to taste

Instructions:

1. Preheat the oven to 400°F (200°C).
2. Place the eggplant slices on a baking sheet.
3. In a small bowl, mix tahini, olive oil, minced garlic, salt, and pepper.
4. Brush the eggplant slices with the tahini mixture on both sides.
5. Roast in the oven for 10-12 minutes or until golden brown.

Nutritional Information (per serving):
Cal: 200 | Carbs: 18g | Pro: 4g | Fat: 14g
Sugars: 8g | Fiber: 10g

15. Quinoa & Black Bean Bell Peppers

Preparation time: 15 minutes
Servings: 2

Ingredients:

- 1 cup cooked quinoa
- 1 cup black beans, drained and rinsed
- 1 cup diced tomatoes
- 1 teaspoon cumin
- Salt and pepper, to taste
- 2 bell peppers, halved and seeds removed

Instructions:

1. Preheat the oven to 375°F (190°C).
2. In a bowl, mix cooked quinoa, black beans, diced tomatoes, cumin, salt, and pepper.
3. Stuff each bell pepper half with the quinoa mixture.
4. Place the stuffed peppers in a baking dish and cover with foil.
5. Bake for 25-30 minutes or until the peppers are tender.

Nutritional Information (per serving):
Cal: 330 | Carbs: 60g | Pro: 15g | Fat: 3g
Sugars: 6g | Fiber: 15g

16. Turmeric Infused Roasted Potatoes

Preparation time: 10 minutes
Servings: 2

Ingredients:

- 4 medium-sized potatoes, diced
- 2 tablespoons olive oil
- 1 teaspoon ground turmeric
- Salt and pepper, to taste
- Fresh parsley, for garnish (optional)

Instructions:

1. Preheat the oven to 400°F (200°C).
2. In a bowl, toss diced potatoes with olive oil, ground turmeric, salt, and pepper.
3. Spread the potatoes on a baking sheet in a single layer.
4. Roast in the oven for 25-30 minutes or until golden brown and crispy.
5. Garnish with fresh parsley if desired.

Nutritional Information (per serving):
Cal: 280 | Carbs: 50g | Pro: 5g | Fat: 8g
Sugars: 2g | Fiber: 7g

17. Spicy Garlic Sauteed Spinach

Preparation time: 5 minutes
Servings: 2

Ingredients:

- 8 cups fresh spinach leaves
- 2 tablespoons olive oil
- 2 cloves garlic, minced
- Pinch of red pepper flakes (adjust to taste)
- Salt, to taste

Instructions:

1. Heat olive oil in a large skillet over medium heat.
2. Add minced garlic and red pepper flakes, sautéing for 1-2 minutes until fragrant.
3. Add the fresh spinach to the skillet and toss until wilted.
4. Season with salt to taste and continue to sauté for an additional 2-3 minutes.
5. Serve immediately.

Nutritional Information (per serving):
Cal: 140 | Carbs: 10g | Pro: 5g | Fat: 11g
Sugars: 1g | Fiber: 5g

18. Cabbage and Apple Slaw

Preparation time: 10 minutes
Servings: 2

Ingredients:

- 2 cups shredded green cabbage
- 1 apple, thinly sliced
- 2 tablespoons Dijon mustard
- 1 tablespoon olive oil
- 1 tablespoon apple cider vinegar
- Salt and pepper, to taste

Instructions:

1. In a large bowl, combine shredded cabbage and sliced apple.
2. In a small bowl, whisk together Dijon mustard, olive oil, apple cider vinegar, salt, and pepper.
3. Pour the dressing over the cabbage and apple, tossing to coat evenly.
4. Let the slaw sit for a few minutes before serving.

Nutritional Information (per serving):
Cal: 120 | Carbs: 18g | Pro: 1g | Fat: 6g
Sugars: 11g | Fiber: 4g

19. Sautéed Mushrooms with Thyme

Preparation time: 8 minutes
Servings: 2

Ingredients:

- 2 cups sliced mushrooms (any variety)
- 2 tablespoons olive oil
- 2 teaspoons fresh thyme leaves
- 1 clove garlic, minced
- Salt and pepper, to taste

Instructions:

1. Heat olive oil in a skillet over medium-high heat.
2. Add sliced mushrooms to the skillet, sautéing until they release their moisture.
3. Stir in minced garlic and fresh thyme leaves, continuing to sauté for an additional 2-3 minutes.
4. Season with salt and pepper to taste.
5. Serve the sautéed mushrooms warm.

Nutritional Information (per serving):
Cal: 110 | Carbs: 4g | Pro: 3g | Fat: 10g
Sugars: 2g | Fiber: 1g

20. Grilled Artichokes with Lemon Aioli

Preparation time: 15 minutes
Servings: 2

Ingredients:

- 2 large artichokes, halved and choke removed
- 2 tablespoons olive oil
- Juice of 1 lemon
- Salt and pepper, to taste

For Lemon Aioli:

- 1/4 cup mayonnaise (preferably olive oil-based)
- 1 teaspoon lemon zest
- 1 tablespoon lemon juice
- 1 clove garlic, minced
- Salt and pepper, to taste

Instructions:

1. Preheat the grill to medium-high heat.
2. Brush artichoke halves with olive oil and sprinkle with lemon juice, salt, and pepper.
3. Grill the artichokes for 8-10 minutes per side until they develop grill marks.
4. Meanwhile, prepare the lemon aioli by mixing all aioli ingredients in a bowl.
5. Serve grilled artichokes with lemon aioli on the side.

Nutritional Information (per serving):
Cal: 240 | Carbs: 15g | Pro: 2g | Fat: 21g
Sugars: 3g | Fiber: 7g

Soups

1. Turmeric and Lentil Soup

Preparation time: 15 minutes
Servings: 2

Ingredients:

- 1 cup red lentils, rinsed
- 4 cups vegetable broth
- 1 teaspoon ground turmeric
- 1 small onion, finely chopped
- 2 cloves garlic, minced

Instructions:

1. In a medium-sized pot, combine red lentils, vegetable broth, turmeric, chopped onion, and minced garlic.
2. Bring the mixture to a boil over medium-high heat.
3. Reduce heat to low, cover, and let it simmer for about 12-15 minutes or until lentils are tender.
4. Stir occasionally during cooking to prevent sticking.
5. Once lentils are cooked, use an immersion blender to partially blend the soup for a creamier texture, leaving some lentils whole.
6. Season with salt and pepper to taste.
7. Serve hot, garnished with a sprinkle of fresh herbs if desired.

Nutritional Information (per serving):
Cal: 320 | Carbs: 56g | Pro: 21g | Fat: 1g
Sugars: 4g | Fiber: 20g

2. Ginger Carrot Soup with Coconut Milk

Preparation time: 20 minutes
Servings: 2

Ingredients:

- 4 large carrots, peeled and chopped
- 1 can (14 oz) coconut milk
- 1 tablespoon fresh ginger, grated
- 1 small onion, chopped
- 2 cups vegetable broth

Instructions:

1. In a pot, combine chopped carrots, coconut milk, grated ginger, chopped onion, and vegetable broth.
2. Bring the mixture to a boil over medium-high heat.
3. Reduce heat to low, cover, and simmer for about 15-20 minutes or until carrots are tender.
4. Use an immersion blender to blend the soup until smooth.
5. Season with salt and pepper to taste.
6. Serve hot, garnished with a drizzle of coconut milk and a sprinkle of fresh cilantro if desired.

Nutritional Information (per serving):
Cal: 340 | Carbs: 32g | Pro: 4g | Fat: 24g
Sugars: 10g | Fiber: 6g

3. Tomato Basil Quinoa Soup

Preparation time: 20 minutes
Servings: 2

Ingredients:

- 1 cup cooked quinoa
- 1 can (14 oz) diced tomatoes
- 2 cups vegetable broth
- 1 cup fresh basil leaves
- 1 clove garlic, minced

Instructions:

1. In a pot, combine cooked quinoa, diced tomatoes, vegetable broth, fresh basil leaves, and minced garlic.
2. Bring the mixture to a simmer over medium heat.
3. Let it simmer for about 10-15 minutes to allow flavors to meld.
4. Season with salt and pepper to taste.
5. Serve hot, garnished with additional fresh basil if desired.

Nutritional Information (per serving):
Cal: 240 | Carbs: 48g | Pro: 8g | Fat: 2g
Sugars: 7g | Fiber: 8g

4. Spicy Kale & Chickpea Soup

Preparation time: 15 minutes
Servings: 2

Ingredients:

- 2 cups chopped kale
- 1 can (14 oz) chickpeas, drained and rinsed

- 4 cups vegetable broth
- 1 teaspoon chili flakes
- 1 tablespoon olive oil

Instructions:

1. In a pot, heat olive oil over medium heat.
2. Add chopped kale and sauté for 2-3 minutes until slightly wilted.
3. Add chickpeas, vegetable broth, and chili flakes to the pot.
4. Bring the mixture to a boil, then reduce heat and simmer for 10 minutes.
5. Season with salt and pepper to taste.
6. Serve hot, optionally drizzled with a bit of olive oil.

Nutritional Information (per serving):
Cal: 280 | Carbs: 40g | Pro: 14g | Fat: 8g
Sugars: 8g | Fiber: 14g

5. Lemon Garlic Chicken Soup

Preparation time: 20 minutes
Servings: 2

Ingredients:

- 2 boneless, skinless chicken breasts, cooked and shredded
- 4 cups chicken broth
- 1 lemon, juiced
- 2 cloves garlic, minced
- 1 cup baby spinach leaves

Instructions:

1. In a pot, combine shredded chicken, chicken broth, lemon juice, and minced garlic.
2. Bring the mixture to a simmer over medium heat.
3. Add baby spinach and let it simmer for an additional 5 minutes until the spinach wilts.
4. Season with salt and pepper to taste.
5. Serve hot, garnished with a slice of lemon if desired.

Nutritional Information (per serving):
Cal: 180 | Carbs: 5g | Pro: 30g | Fat: 3g
Sugars: 1g | Fiber: 1g

6. Butternut Squash and Apple Soup

Preparation time: 25 minutes
Servings: 2

Ingredients:

- 2 cups butternut squash, peeled and cubed
- 1 apple, peeled and chopped
- 4 cups vegetable broth
- 1 teaspoon ground cinnamon
- 1 tablespoon olive oil

Instructions:

1. In a pot, heat olive oil over medium heat.
2. Add cubed butternut squash and chopped apple, sauté for 5 minutes.
3. Pour in vegetable broth and add ground cinnamon.
4. Bring the mixture to a boil, then reduce heat and let it simmer for 15-20 minutes or until squash is tender.
5. Use an immersion blender to blend the soup until smooth.
6. Season with salt and pepper to taste.
7. Serve hot, optionally garnished with a sprinkle of cinnamon.

Nutritional Information (per serving):
Cal: 230 | Carbs: 48g | Pro: 3g | Fat: 5g
Sugars: 18g | Fiber: 7g

7. Thai Coconut Shrimp Soup

Preparation time: 20 minutes
Servings: 2

Ingredients:

- 8 oz shrimp, peeled and deveined
- 1 can (14 oz) coconut milk
- 1 tablespoon red curry paste
- 1 cup sliced mushrooms
- 1 stalk lemongrass, bruised

Instructions:

1. In a pot, combine coconut milk, red curry paste, sliced mushrooms, and lemongrass.
2. Bring the mixture to a simmer over medium heat.
3. Add shrimp and let it simmer for 5-7 minutes or until shrimp are cooked through.
4. Remove lemongrass before serving.
5. Season with salt to taste.
6. Serve hot, garnished with fresh cilantro if desired.

Nutritional Information (per serving):
Cal: 380 | Carbs: 7g | Pro: 18g | Fat: 32g
Sugars: 2g | Fiber: 1g

8. Spinach and White Bean Soup

Preparation time: 15 minutes
Servings: 2

Ingredients:

- 2 cups fresh spinach leaves
- 1 can (14 oz) white beans, drained and rinsed
- 4 cups vegetable broth
- 1 onion, chopped
- 2 cloves garlic, minced

Instructions:

1. In a pot, sauté chopped onion and minced garlic over medium heat until softened.
2. Add vegetable broth, white beans, and fresh spinach to the pot.
3. Bring the mixture to a boil, then reduce heat and let it simmer for 10 minutes.
4. Season with salt and pepper to taste.
5. Serve hot, optionally garnished with a sprinkle of nutritional yeast.

Nutritional Information (per serving):
Cal: 260 | Carbs: 42g | Pro: 15g | Fat: 2g
Sugars: 4g | Fiber: 12g

9. Broccoli and Turmeric Soup

Preparation time: 20 minutes
Servings: 2

Ingredients:

- 2 cups broccoli florets
- 1 teaspoon ground turmeric
- 4 cups vegetable broth
- 1 onion, chopped
- 2 tablespoons olive oil

Instructions:

1. In a pot, heat olive oil over medium heat.
2. Add chopped onion and sauté until translucent.
3. Add broccoli, ground turmeric, and vegetable broth to the pot.
4. Bring the mixture to a boil, then reduce heat and let it simmer for 15 minutes or until broccoli is tender.
5. Use an immersion blender to blend the soup until smooth.
6. Season with salt and pepper to taste.
7. Serve hot, optionally garnished with a drizzle of olive oil.

Nutritional Information (per serving):
Cal: 180 | Carbs: 20g | Pro: 6g | Fat: 10g
Sugars: 5g | Fiber: 6g

10. Moroccan Spiced Lentil Soup

Preparation time: 20 minutes
Servings: 2

Ingredients:

- 1 cup dried green lentils, rinsed
- 4 cups vegetable broth
- 1 can (14 oz) diced tomatoes
- 1 teaspoon Moroccan spice blend
- 1 carrot, diced

Instructions:

1. In a pot, combine dried green lentils, vegetable broth, diced tomatoes, Moroccan spice blend, and diced carrot.
2. Bring the mixture to a boil over medium-high heat.
3. Reduce heat to low, cover, and let it simmer for about 15-20 minutes or until lentils are tender.
4. Stir occasionally during cooking to prevent sticking.
5. Season with salt and pepper to taste.
6. Serve hot, garnished with a squeeze of lemon if desired.

Nutritional Information (per serving):
Cal: 320 | Carbs: 56g | Pro: 22g | Fat: 1g
Sugars: 5g | Fiber: 20g

11. Creamy Cauliflower & Leek Soup

Preparation time: 15 minutes
Servings: 2

Ingredients:

- 1 medium cauliflower, chopped

- 1 leek, sliced
- 2 cups vegetable broth
- 1 cup unsweetened almond milk
- Salt and pepper to taste

Instructions:

1. In a pot, combine cauliflower, leek, and vegetable broth.
2. Bring the mixture to a boil, then reduce heat and simmer until cauliflower is tender (about 10 minutes).
3. Use an immersion blender to blend the soup until smooth.
4. Stir in almond milk and season with salt and pepper to taste.
5. Simmer for an additional 5 minutes, ensuring the soup is heated through.
6. Serve hot, and enjoy the creamy goodness!

Nutritional Information (per serving):
Cal: 120 | Carbs: 21g | Pro: 5g | Fat: 3g
Sugars: 7g | Fiber: 7g

12. Chicken and Vegetable Detox Soup

Preparation time: 20 minutes
Servings: 2

Ingredients:

- 1 chicken breast, cooked and shredded
- 2 cups mixed vegetables (carrots, broccoli, kale)
- 4 cups chicken broth
- 1 teaspoon turmeric powder
- Salt and pepper to taste

Instructions:

1. In a pot, combine shredded chicken, mixed vegetables, chicken broth, and turmeric powder.
2. Bring to a boil, then reduce heat and simmer until vegetables are tender (about 15 minutes).
3. Season with salt and pepper to taste.
4. Allow flavors to meld by simmering for an additional 5 minutes.
5. Serve hot for a comforting and detoxifying meal!

Nutritional Information (per serving):
Cal: 180 | Carbs: 15g | Pro: 20g | Fat: 4g
Sugars: 4g | Fiber: 5g

13. Tom Yum Soup with Shrimp

Preparation time: 15 minutes
Servings: 2

Ingredients:

- 8 oz shrimp, peeled and deveined
- 4 cups vegetable broth
- 1 lemongrass stalk, smashed
- 2 kaffir lime leaves
- 2 tablespoons fish sauce

Instructions:

1. In a pot, bring vegetable broth, lemongrass, and kaffir lime leaves to a simmer.
2. Add shrimp and cook until they turn pink and opaque.
3. Stir in fish sauce and let the flavors meld for an additional 5 minutes.
4. Remove lemongrass and lime leaves before serving.
5. Enjoy the aromatic and tangy Tom Yum soup!

Nutritional Information (per serving):
Cal: 150 | Carbs: 4g | Pro: 24g | Fat: 3g
Sugars: 1g | Fiber: 0g

14. Quinoa Minestrone Soup

Preparation time: 20 minutes
Servings: 2

Ingredients:

- 1/2 cup quinoa, rinsed
- 4 cups vegetable broth
- 1 cup diced tomatoes
- 1 cup mixed vegetables (carrots, celery, zucchini)
- Italian seasoning to taste

Instructions:

1. In a pot, combine quinoa, vegetable broth, tomatoes, and mixed vegetables.
2. Season with Italian seasoning to taste.
3. Bring to a boil, then reduce heat and simmer until quinoa is cooked and vegetables are tender (about 15 minutes).
4. Adjust seasoning if needed and serve hot for a hearty meal!

Nutritional Information (per serving):
Cal: 220 | Carbs: 38g | Pro: 8g | Fat: 4g
Sugars: 6g | Fiber: 7g

15. Roasted Red Pepper & Tomato Soup

Preparation time: 25 minutes
Servings: 2

Ingredients:

- 2 large red bell peppers, roasted and peeled
- 1 can (14 oz) diced tomatoes
- 1 onion, chopped
- 2 cups vegetable broth
- Olive oil for roasting

Instructions:

1. Roast red peppers in the oven until skin blisters. Peel and chop.
2. In a pot, sauté chopped onion until translucent.
3. Add roasted red peppers, diced tomatoes, and vegetable broth.
4. Simmer for 15 minutes, allowing flavors to meld.
5. Blend the soup until smooth using an immersion blender.
6. Serve hot, drizzling with a touch of olive oil.

Nutritional Information (per serving):
Cal: 150 | Carbs: 30g | Pro: 5g | Fat: 2g
Sugars: 15g | Fiber: 7g

16. Miso Soup with Tofu and Seaweed

Preparation time: 15 minutes
Servings: 2

Ingredients:

- 2 tablespoons miso paste
- 4 cups vegetable broth
- 1 cup firm tofu, cubed
- 2 sheets nori seaweed, shredded
- Green onions for garnish

Instructions:

1. In a pot, whisk miso paste into vegetable broth until dissolved.
2. Bring to a gentle simmer.
3. Add tofu cubes and shredded nori seaweed.
4. Simmer for 10 minutes, ensuring tofu is heated through.
5. Garnish with green onions before serving.

Nutritional Information (per serving):
Cal: 110 | Carbs: 9g | Pro: 10g | Fat: 5g
Sugars: 2g | Fiber: 2g

17. Black Bean and Vegetable Chili

Preparation time: 30 minutes
Servings: 2

Ingredients:

- 1 can (15 oz) black beans, drained and rinsed
- 1 cup diced tomatoes
- 1 cup mixed vegetables (bell peppers, corn, onions)
- 2 teaspoons chili powder
- 1 cup vegetable broth

Instructions:

1. In a pot, combine black beans, diced tomatoes, mixed vegetables, chili powder.
2. Pour in vegetable broth and bring to a boil.
3. Reduce heat and simmer for 20 minutes.
4. Adjust seasoning if needed and serve hot.
5. Enjoy this protein-packed and flavorful chili!

Nutritional Information (per serving):
Cal: 250 | Carbs: 46g | Pro: 14g | Fat: 1g
Sugars: 8g | Fiber: 14g

18. Lemon Chicken Orzo Soup

Preparation time: 25 minutes
Servings: 2

Ingredients:

- 1 chicken breast, cooked and shredded
- 1/2 cup orzo pasta
- 4 cups chicken broth
- Juice of 1 lemon
- Fresh dill for garnish

Instructions:

1. In a pot, combine shredded chicken, orzo pasta, and chicken broth.
2. Bring to a boil, then reduce heat and simmer

until orzo is cooked.
3. Stir in lemon juice and simmer for an additional 5 minutes.
4. Garnish with fresh dill before serving.

Nutritional Information (per serving):
Cal: 220 | Carbs: 22g | Pro: 23g | Fat: 3g
Sugars: 1g | Fiber: 2g

19. Spiced Pumpkin Soup

Preparation time: 30 minutes
Servings: 2

Ingredients:

- 2 cups pumpkin puree
- 4 cups vegetable broth
- 1 teaspoon ground cinnamon
- 1/2 teaspoon ground nutmeg
- 2 tablespoons pepitas (pumpkin seeds) for garnish

Instructions:

1. In a pot, combine pumpkin puree, vegetable broth, cinnamon, and nutmeg.
2. Bring to a gentle simmer for 20 minutes.
3. Blend the soup until smooth using an immersion blender.
4. Toast pepitas in a dry pan until golden.
5. Serve the soup hot, garnished with toasted pepitas.

Nutritional Information (per serving):
Cal: 160 | Carbs: 32g | Pro: 4g | Fat: 2g
Sugars: 14g | Fiber: 8g

20. Cabbage & Turmeric Detox Soup

Preparation time: 20 minutes
Servings: 2

Ingredients:

- 2 cups shredded cabbage
- 1 cup carrots, julienned
- 4 cups vegetable broth
- 1 teaspoon ground turmeric
- Salt and pepper to taste

Instructions:

1. In a pot, combine shredded cabbage, julienned carrots, vegetable broth, and turmeric.
2. Bring to a boil, then reduce heat and simmer until vegetables are tender.
3. Season with salt and pepper to taste.
4. Simmer for an additional 5 minutes.
5. Serve hot for a refreshing and detoxifying meal.

Nutritional Information (per serving):
Cal: 80 | Carbs: 18g | Pro: 2g | Fat: 0g
Sugars: 9g | Fiber: 4g

Vegetarian

1. Vegetable & Quinoa Stuffed Peppers

Preparation time: 15 minutes
Servings: 2

Ingredients:

- 2 large bell peppers, halved and seeds removed
- 1 cup cooked quinoa
- 1 cup mixed roasted vegetables (zucchini, cherry tomatoes, and red onion)
- 1 tablespoon olive oil
- Salt and pepper to taste

Instructions:

1. Preheat the oven to 375°F (190°C).
2. In a mixing bowl, combine cooked quinoa and roasted vegetables.
3. Drizzle olive oil over the quinoa and vegetable mixture. Season with salt and pepper. Toss to combine.
4. Place the bell pepper halves on a baking sheet.
5. Stuff each pepper half with the quinoa and vegetable mixture.
6. Bake in the preheated oven for 20-25 minutes or until the peppers are tender.
7. Remove from the oven and let them cool for a few minutes before serving.

Nutritional Information (per serving):
Cal: 230 | Carbs: 35g | Pro: 6g | Fat: 8g
Sugars: 6g | Fiber: 7g

2. Lentil and Sweet Potato Curry

Preparation time: 20 minutes
Servings: 2

Ingredients:

- 1 cup dry green lentils, rinsed
- 1 large sweet potato, peeled and diced
- 1 can (14 oz) diced tomatoes
- 1 tablespoon curry powder
- Salt to taste

Instructions:

1. In a pot, combine lentils, sweet potato, diced tomatoes (with juice), and curry powder.
2. Add enough water to cover the ingredients. Bring to a boil.
3. Reduce heat and let it simmer until lentils and sweet potatoes are tender (about 15-20 minutes).
4. Season with salt to taste.
5. Serve over cooked quinoa or brown rice.

Nutritional Information (per serving):
Cal: 380 | Carbs: 70g | Pro: 21g | Fat: 1g
Sugars: 10g | Fiber: 20g

3. Chickpea & Spinach Coconut Curry

Preparation time: 15 minutes
Servings: 2

Ingredients:

- 1 can (15 oz) chickpeas, drained and rinsed
- 2 cups fresh spinach
- 1 can (14 oz) coconut milk
- 1 tablespoon curry paste
- Salt to taste

Instructions:

1. In a pan, combine chickpeas, fresh spinach, coconut milk, and curry paste.
2. Bring to a simmer and cook until the spinach wilts.
3. Season with salt to taste.
4. Serve over quinoa or brown rice.

Nutritional Information (per serving):
Cal: 480 | Carbs: 45g | Pro: 16g | Fat: 30g
Sugars: 2g | Fiber: 12g

4. Eggplant and Tomato Caponata

Preparation time: 15 minutes
Servings: 2

Ingredients:

- 1 medium eggplant, diced
- 1 cup cherry tomatoes, halved
- 2 tablespoons olive oil
- 2 cloves garlic, minced
- Fresh basil leaves for garnish

Instructions:

1. Heat olive oil in a pan over medium heat. Add minced garlic and sauté until fragrant.
2. Add diced eggplant and cook until softened.

3. Stir in cherry tomatoes and cook until they release their juices.
4. Season with salt and pepper to taste.
5. Garnish with fresh basil leaves before serving.

Nutritional Information (per serving):
Cal: 180 | Carbs: 20g | Pro: 3g | Fat: 11g
Sugars: 10g | Fiber: 7g

5. Grilled Portobello Mushrooms

Preparation time: 10 minutes
Servings: 2

Ingredients:

- 4 large Portobello mushrooms, cleaned
- 2 tablespoons balsamic glaze
- 2 tablespoons olive oil
- Salt and pepper to taste
- Fresh thyme leaves for garnish

Instructions:

1. Preheat the grill or grill pan over medium-high heat.
2. Brush Portobello mushrooms with olive oil and season with salt and pepper.
3. Grill mushrooms for 4-5 minutes per side until tender.
4. Drizzle balsamic glaze over the grilled mushrooms.
5. Garnish with fresh thyme leaves before serving.

Nutritional Information (per serving):
Cal: 120 | Carbs: 10g | Pro: 4g | Fat: 8g
Sugars: 5g | Fiber: 4g

6. Quinoa & Black Bean Veggie Burgers

Preparation time: 20 minutes
Servings: 2

Ingredients:

- 1 cup cooked quinoa
- 1 can (15 oz) black beans, drained and rinsed
- 1/2 cup finely chopped red onion
- 1 teaspoon cumin
- Salt and pepper to taste

Instructions:

1. In a bowl, mash black beans with a fork.
2. Add cooked quinoa, chopped red onion, cumin, salt, and pepper. Mix well.
3. Form the mixture into patties.
4. Cook on a grill or stovetop for 3-4 minutes per side.
5. Serve in whole-grain buns with your favorite toppings.

Nutritional Information (per serving):
Cal: 280 | Carbs: 52g | Pro: 14g | Fat: 3g
Sugars: 3g | Fiber: 12g

7. Spinach & Feta Stuffed Mushrooms

Preparation time: 15 minutes
Servings: 2

Ingredients:

- 8 large button mushrooms, cleaned and stems removed
- 2 cups fresh spinach, chopped
- 1/2 cup crumbled feta cheese
- 2 cloves garlic, minced
- Olive oil for brushing

Instructions:

1. Preheat the oven to 375°F (190°C).
2. In a pan, sauté chopped spinach and minced garlic until wilted.
3. Fill each mushroom cap with the sautéed spinach.
4. Top with crumbled feta cheese.
5. Brush mushrooms with olive oil and bake for 15-20 minutes.

Nutritional Information (per serving):
Cal: 150 | Carbs: 9g | Pro: 9g | Fat: 10g
Sugars: 3g | Fiber: 3g

8. Ratatouille with Herbs de Provence

Preparation time: 20 minutes
Servings: 2

Ingredients:

- 1 medium eggplant, diced
- 1 zucchini, diced
- 1 bell pepper, diced
- 1 cup cherry tomatoes, halved
- 2 tablespoons olive oil

- 1 teaspoon Herbs de Provence
- Salt and pepper to taste

Instructions:

1. Preheat the oven to 375°F (190°C).
2. In a baking dish, combine diced eggplant, zucchini, bell pepper, and cherry tomatoes.
3. Drizzle olive oil over the vegetables, sprinkle with Herbs de Provence, salt, and pepper. Toss to coat.
4. Roast in the oven for 20-25 minutes or until vegetables are tender.

Nutritional Information (per serving):
Cal: 180 | Carbs: 20g | Pro: 3g | Fat: 11g
Sugars: 10g | Fiber: 7g

9. Cauliflower Steak

Preparation time: 15 minutes
Servings: 2

Ingredients:

- 1 large cauliflower head, sliced into steaks
- 2 tablespoons olive oil
- Salt and pepper to taste
- 1 cup fresh parsley, finely chopped
- 3 cloves garlic, minced
- 1/4 cup red wine vinegar

Instructions:

1. Preheat the oven to 400°F (200°C).
2. Brush cauliflower steaks with olive oil and season with salt and pepper.
3. Roast in the oven for 20-25 minutes or until golden brown.
4. In a bowl, combine chopped parsley, minced garlic, and red wine vinegar to make chimichurri sauce.
5. Drizzle chimichurri sauce over roasted cauliflower steaks before serving.

Nutritional Information (per serving):
Cal: 160 | Carbs: 15g | Pro: 5g | Fat: 11g
Sugars: 5g | Fiber: 7g

10. Sweet Potato & Black Bean Enchiladas

Preparation time: 25 minutes
Servings: 2

Ingredients:

- 4 small whole-grain tortillas
- 1 large sweet potato, cooked and mashed
- 1 can (15 oz) black beans, drained and rinsed
- 1 cup salsa
- 1/2 cup shredded plant-based cheese

Instructions:

1. Preheat the oven to 375°F (190°C).
2. In a bowl, mix mashed sweet potato and black beans.
3. Fill each tortilla with the sweet potato and black bean mixture.
4. Roll tortillas and place them in a baking dish.
5. Pour salsa over the enchiladas and sprinkle with shredded cheese.
6. Bake for 15-20 minutes or until the cheese is melted and bubbly.

Nutritional Information (per serving):
Cal: 420 | Carbs: 70g | Pro: 18g | Fat: 7g
Sugars: 10g | Fiber: 14g

11. Zucchini Noodles

Preparation time: 15 minutes
Servings: 2

Ingredients:

- 2 medium-sized zucchinis, spiralized
- 1 cup cherry tomatoes, halved
- 1/4 cup homemade or store-bought pesto
- 2 tablespoons extra-virgin olive oil
- Salt and pepper to taste

Instructions:

1. In a large pan, heat olive oil over medium heat.
2. Add spiralized zucchini noodles and sauté for 3-4 minutes until just tender, stirring occasionally.
3. Add cherry tomatoes to the pan and continue to sauté for an additional 2-3 minutes.
4. Stir in pesto, ensuring the zucchini noodles and cherry tomatoes are evenly coated.
5. Season with salt and pepper to taste.
6. Cook for an additional 1-2 minutes until everything is heated through.
7. Divide the zucchini noodle mixture between two plates and serve immediately.

Nutritional Information (per serving):
Cal: 245 | Carbs: 10g | Pro: 4g | Fat: 22g
Sugars: 6g | Fiber: 3g

12. Mediterranean Chickpea Patties

Preparation time: 20 minutes
Servings: 2

Ingredients:

- 1 can (15 oz) chickpeas, drained and rinsed
- 1/4 cup chopped red onion
- 2 tablespoons chopped fresh parsley
- 1 teaspoon ground cumin
- Olive oil for cooking

Instructions:

1. In a food processor, combine chickpeas, red onion, parsley, and cumin.
2. Pulse until well combined but still slightly chunky.
3. Form the mixture into four small patties.
4. Heat olive oil in a pan over medium heat.
5. Cook the chickpea patties for 3-4 minutes per side until golden brown.
6. Serve the patties on a plate with your favorite salad or whole grains.

Nutritional Information (per serving):
Cal: 255 | Carbs: 38g | Pro: 12g | Fat: 7g
Sugars: 7g | Fiber: 11g

13. Red Pepper & Spinach Quesadillas

Preparation time: 15 minutes
Servings: 2

Ingredients:

- 4 whole-grain tortillas
- 1 cup fresh spinach leaves
- 1/2 cup jarred roasted red peppers, drained and sliced
- 1 cup shredded mozzarella cheese
- Olive oil for cooking

Instructions:

1. Place two tortillas on a clean surface.
2. Layer each tortilla with fresh spinach, roasted red peppers, and shredded mozzarella.
3. Top with the remaining two tortillas to create quesadillas.
4. Heat olive oil in a pan over medium heat.
5. Cook each quesadilla for 2-3 minutes on each side until the cheese is melted and the tortillas are golden brown.
6. Remove from the pan, let them cool for a minute, and then cut into wedges.
7. Serve warm.

Nutritional Information (per serving):
Cal: 380 | Carbs: 40g | Pro: 17g | Fat: 17g
Sugars: 4g | Fiber: 6g

14. Wild Mushroom Risotto

Preparation time: 25 minutes
Servings: 2

Ingredients:

- 1 cup Arborio rice
- 4 cups vegetable broth, heated
- 1 cup mixed wild mushrooms, sliced
- 1/2 cup dry white wine
- 2 tablespoons olive oil
- Salt and pepper to taste

Instructions:

1. In a large pan, heat olive oil over medium heat.
2. Add sliced wild mushrooms and sauté for 5 minutes until golden brown.
3. Stir in Arborio rice and cook for an additional 2 minutes.
4. Pour in the white wine and cook until mostly evaporated.
5. Begin adding the heated vegetable broth, one ladle at a time, stirring frequently until absorbed before adding more.
6. Continue this process until the rice is creamy and cooked to al dente.
7. Season with salt and pepper to taste.
8. Divide the risotto between two plates and serve immediately.

Nutritional Information (per serving):
Cal: 410 | Carbs: 70g | Pro: 8g | Fat: 10g
Sugars: 2g | Fiber: 3g

15. Stuffed Acorn Squash

Preparation time: 30 minutes
Servings: 2

Ingredients:

- 1 acorn squash, halved and seeds removed
- 1 cup cooked quinoa
- 1/4 cup dried cranberries
- 2 tablespoons chopped pecans
- 1 tablespoon maple syrup
- Cinnamon for sprinkling

Instructions:

1. Preheat the oven to 400°F (200°C).
2. Place acorn squash halves on a baking sheet, cut side up.
3. In a bowl, mix cooked quinoa, dried cranberries, chopped pecans, maple syrup.
4. Spoon the quinoa mixture into each acorn squash half.
5. Sprinkle cinnamon over the top.
6. Bake for 25-30 minutes or until the squash is tender.
7. Serve warm.

Nutritional Information (per serving):
Cal: 380 | Carbs: 75g | Pro: 7g | Fat: 7g
Sugars: 15g | Fiber: 9g

16. Spinach & Artichoke Stuffed Portobellos

Preparation time: 20 minutes
Servings: 2

Ingredients:

- 4 large portobello mushrooms, stems removed
- 1 cup fresh spinach, chopped
- 1/2 cup canned artichoke hearts, drained and chopped
- 1/2 cup cream cheese (dairy or plant-based)
- 2 tablespoons grated Parmesan cheese (optional)

Instructions:

1. Preheat the oven to 375°F (190°C).
2. Place portobello mushrooms on a baking sheet.
3. In a bowl, mix chopped spinach, artichoke hearts, and cream cheese.
4. Divide the mixture evenly among the portobello mushrooms.
5. Sprinkle grated Parmesan cheese on top if desired.
6. Bake for 15-18 minutes or until mushrooms are tender and filling is hot.
7. Serve immediately.

Nutritional Information (per serving):
Cal: 250 | Carbs: 20g | Pro: 10g | Fat: 15g
Sugars: 5g | Fiber: 7g

17. Turmeric Coconut Chickpea Stew

Preparation time: 25 minutes
Servings: 2

Ingredients:

- 1 can (15 oz) chickpeas, drained and rinsed
- 1 cup coconut milk (full-fat or light)
- 1 cup cherry tomatoes, halved
- 1 teaspoon ground turmeric
- 2 tablespoons fresh cilantro, chopped
- Salt and pepper to taste

Instructions:

1. In a pot, combine chickpeas, coconut milk, cherry tomatoes, and turmeric.
2. Bring to a simmer over medium heat.
3. Cook for 15-20 minutes, allowing flavors to meld.
4. Season with salt and pepper to taste.
5. Serve the stew in bowls, garnished with fresh cilantro.

Nutritional Information (per serving):
Cal: 380 | Carbs: 44g | Pro: 14g | Fat: 18g
Sugars: 10g | Fiber: 11g

18. Pesto Zoodles with Cherry Tomatoes

Preparation time: 15 minutes
Servings: 2

Ingredients:

- 4 medium zucchinis, spiralized
- 1/2 cup cherry tomatoes, halved
- 1/4 cup homemade or store-bought pesto
- 2 tablespoons pine nuts, toasted
- Salt and pepper to taste

Instructions:

1. In a large bowl, toss spiralized zucchini with cherry tomatoes.
2. Add pesto and mix until well combined.

3. Season with salt and pepper to taste.
4. Top with toasted pine nuts just before serving.
5. Serve immediately.

Nutritional Information (per serving):
Cal: 220 | Carbs: 15g | Pro: 5g | Fat: 16g
Sugars: 7g | Fiber: 4g

19. Butternut Squash & Sage Risotto

Preparation time: 30 minutes
Servings: 2

Ingredients:

- 1 cup Arborio rice
- 3 cups vegetable broth, heated
- 1 cup butternut squash, diced
- 1 tablespoon olive oil
- Fresh sage leaves for garnish
- Salt and pepper to taste

Instructions:

1. In a large pan, heat olive oil over medium heat.
2. Add diced butternut squash and sauté until slightly golden.
3. Stir in Arborio rice and cook for an additional 2 minutes.
4. Begin adding the heated vegetable broth, one ladle at a time, stirring frequently until absorbed before adding more.
5. Continue this process until the rice is creamy and cooked to al dente.
6. Season with salt and pepper to taste.
7. Garnish with fresh sage leaves before serving.

Nutritional Information (per serving):
Cal: 390 | Carbs: 80g | Pro: 6g | Fat: 5g
Sugars: 2g | Fiber: 5g

20. Greek-Style Roasted Vegetables

Preparation time: 25 minutes
Servings: 2

Ingredients:

- 1 cup cherry tomatoes, halved
- 1 cup bell peppers, sliced
- 1 cup zucchini, sliced
- 1 red onion, sliced
- 2 tablespoons olive oil
- 1/2 cup crumbled feta cheese
- Fresh oregano for garnish
- Salt and pepper to taste

Instructions:

1. Preheat the oven to 400°F (200°C).
2. In a large bowl, toss cherry tomatoes, bell peppers, zucchini, and red onion with olive oil.
3. Spread the vegetables on a baking sheet in a single layer.
4. Roast for 20-25 minutes or until vegetables are tender and slightly caramelized.
5. Season with salt and pepper to taste.
6. Transfer the roasted vegetables to a serving plate.
7. Sprinkle crumbled feta cheese on top and garnish with fresh oregano.
8. Serve warm.

Nutritional Information (per serving):
Cal: 280 | Carbs: 18g | Pro: 8g | Fat: 21g
Sugars: 8g | Fiber: 5g

Meal Plan

DAY	BREAKFAST	LUNCH	DINNER
1	Turmeric Scrambled Eggs with Spinach	Mediterranean Chickpea Salad with Feta	Baked Salmon with Lemon and Dill
2	Quinoa Breakfast Bowl with Berries and Almonds	Zucchini Noodles with Pesto and Cherry Tomatoes	Lentil and Sweet Potato Curry
3	Avocado Toast with Smoked Salmon	Lemon Herb Baked Cod	Turmeric and Garlic Roasted Chicken
4	Chia Seed Pudding with Mixed Berries	Spinach and Artichoke Stuffed Portobellos	Spinach, Avocado, and Strawberry Salad
5	Oatmeal with Walnuts and Blueberries	Butternut Squash and Sage Risotto	Chickpea and Spinach Coconut Curry
6	Sweet Potato and Kale Breakfast Hash	Quinoa and Roasted Vegetable Salad	Grilled Swordfish with Mango Salsa
7	Greek Yogurt Parfait with Granola and Mango	Roasted Red Pepper and Spinach Quesadillas	Garlic and Herb Grilled Turkey Tenderloin
8	Salmon and Spinach Omelette	Cucumber and Tomato Salad with Olive Oil Dressing	Quinoa Breakfast Bowl with Berries and Almonds
9	Green Smoothie Bowl with Kale and Pineapple	Shrimp and Avocado Salad with Lime Dressing	Roasted Vegetable and Quinoa Stuffed Peppers
10	Almond Flour Pancakes with Berries	Tuna Salad with Avocado and Chickpeas	Tomato Basil Quinoa Soup
11	Coconut and Berry Overnight Oats	Turmeric Coconut Chickpea Stew	Grilled Chicken and Mixed Greens Salad
12	Veggie Frittata with Turmeric	Asian-Inspired Quinoa Salad	Pesto Zoodles with Cherry Tomatoes
13	Buckwheat Pancakes with Greek Yogurt	Baked Haddock with Roasted Vegetables	Avocado, Grapefruit, and Shrimp Salad
14	Banana Walnut Muffins with Flaxseeds	Coconut-Curry Chicken Stir-Fry	Roasted Sweet Potato Wedges
15	Spinach and Mushroom Breakfast Wrap	Seared Tuna with Sesame Ginger Sauce	Greek Salad with Salmon
16	Quinoa Porridge with Cinnamon and Apples	Spicy Grilled Salmon with Avocado Salsa	Lemon Herb Quinoa Pilaf
17	Blueberry and Almond Smoothie	Spinach, Avocado, and Strawberry Salad	Quinoa and Black Bean Veggie Burgers
18	Smashed Avocado and Tomato on Whole Grain Toast	Grilled Zucchini and Tomato Salad	Pesto Grilled Scallop Skewers
19	Berry Protein Smoothie with Hemp Seeds	Roasted Beet and Goat Cheese Salad	Basil and Lemon Roasted Turkey Breast
20	Shakshuka with Spinach and Feta	Mango and Black Bean Salad with Lime Vinaigrette	Miso-Glazed Black Cod
21	Quinoa Breakfast Bowl with Berries and Almonds	Lemon Garlic Chicken Skillet	Roasted Eggplant with Tahini Dressing
22	Avocado Toast with Smoked Salmon	Balsamic Glazed Chicken and Brussels Sprouts	Grilled Artichokes with Lemon Aioli
23	Oatmeal with Walnuts and Blueberries	Honey Mustard Roasted Chicken Wings	Lemon Dill Cucumber Salad
24	Sweet Potato and Kale Breakfast Hash	Mediterranean Turkey Meatballs with Tzatziki	Creamy Cauliflower and Leek Soup
25	Greek Yogurt Parfait with Granola and Mango	Lemon Herb Grilled Chicken Breasts	Black Bean and Vegetable Chili
26	Salmon and Spinach Omelette	Pesto Chicken and Vegetable Kebabs	Turmeric and Lentil Soup
27	Green Smoothie Bowl with Kale and Pineapple	Rosemary and Dijon Mustard Baked Chicken	Spinach and Orange Salad with Walnuts
28	Almond Flour Pancakes with Berries	Grilled Chicken and Vegetable Lettuce Wraps	Tomato Basil Quinoa Soup

DAY	BREAKFAST	LUNCH	DINNER
29	Coconut and Berry Overnight Oats	Spinach and White Bean Soup	Grilled Zucchini and Tomato Salad
30	Veggie Frittata with Turmeric	Roasted Sweet Potato and Kale Salad	Baked Salmon with Lemon and Dill
31	Buckwheat Pancakes with Greek Yogurt	Teriyaki Glazed Salmon	Cabbage and Turmeric Detox Soup
32	Banana Walnut Muffins with Flaxseeds	Grilled Swordfish with Mango Salsa	Spinach and Mushroom Breakfast Wrap
33	Spinach and Artichoke Stuffed Portobellos	Mediterranean Baked Halibut	Coconut-Curry Chicken Stir-Fry
34	Turmeric Coconut Chickpea Stew	Chickpea and Spinach Coconut Curry	Lentil and Sweet Potato Curry
35	Pesto Zoodles with Cherry Tomatoes	Basil and Lemon Roasted Turkey Breast	Shrimp and Avocado Salad with Lime Dressing
36	Butternut Squash and Sage Risotto	Grilled Chicken and Mixed Greens Salad	Quinoa Breakfast Bowl with Berries and Almonds
37	Greek-Style Roasted Vegetables with Feta	Tomato Basil Quinoa Soup	Roasted Sweet Potato Wedges
38	Quinoa Porridge with Cinnamon and Apples	Quinoa and Black Bean Veggie Burgers	Grilled Artichokes with Lemon Aioli
39	Blueberry and Almond Smoothie	Lemon Herb Baked Cod	Roasted Vegetable and Quinoa Stuffed Peppers
40	Smashed Avocado and Tomato on Whole Grain Toast	Roasted Beet and Goat Cheese Salad	Turmeric and Garlic Roasted Chicken
41	Berry Protein Smoothie with Hemp Seeds	Grilled Zucchini and Tomato Salad	Spinach and Orange Salad with Walnuts
42	Shakshuka with Spinach and Feta	Miso-Glazed Black Cod	Coconut and Berry Overnight Oats
43	Quinoa Breakfast Bowl with Berries and Almonds	Pesto Grilled Scallop Skewers	Lemon Garlic Chicken Skillet
44	Avocado Toast with Smoked Salmon	Honey Mustard Roasted Chicken Wings	Spinach, Avocado, and Strawberry Salad
45	Oatmeal with Walnuts and Blueberries	Caprese Salad with Balsamic Glaze	Chickpea and Spinach Coconut Curry
46	Sweet Potato and Kale Breakfast Hash	Spinach and Mushroom Breakfast Wrap	Grilled Swordfish with Mango Salsa
47	Greek Yogurt Parfait with Granola and Mango	Lemon Herb Grilled Chicken Breasts	Basil and Lemon Roasted Turkey Breast
48	Salmon and Spinach Omelette	Grilled Chicken and Vegetable Lettuce Wraps	Tomato Basil Quinoa Soup
49	Green Smoothie Bowl with Kale and Pineapple	Spinach and White Bean Soup	Coconut-Curry Chicken Stir-Fry
50	Almond Flour Pancakes with Berries	Rosemary and Dijon Mustard Baked Chicken	Lentil and Sweet Potato Curry
51	Coconut and Berry Overnight Oats	Teriyaki Glazed Salmon	Roasted Sweet Potato and Kale Salad
52	Veggie Frittata with Turmeric	Pesto Chicken and Vegetable Kebabs	Quinoa Breakfast Bowl with Berries and Almonds
53	Buckwheat Pancakes with Greek Yogurt	Mediterranean Turkey Meatballs with Tzatziki	Shrimp and Avocado Salad with Lime Dressing
54	Banana Walnut Muffins with Flaxseeds	Grilled Swordfish with Mango Salsa	Grilled Zucchini and Tomato Salad
55	Spinach and Artichoke Stuffed Portobellos	Chickpea and Spinach Coconut Curry	Coconut and Berry Overnight Oats

56	Turmeric Coconut Chickpea Stew	Basil and Lemon Roasted Turkey Breast	Lemon Herb Baked Cod
57	Pesto Zoodles with Cherry Tomatoes	Tomato Basil Quinoa Soup	Spinach, Avocado, and Strawberry Salad
58	Butternut Squash and Sage Risotto	Roasted Vegetable and Quinoa Stuffed Peppers	Lentil and Sweet Potato Curry
59	Greek-Style Roasted Vegetables with Feta	Grilled Artichokes with Lemon Aioli	Grilled Swordfish with Mango Salsa
60	Quinoa Porridge with Cinnamon and Apples	Roasted Sweet Potato Wedges	Turmeric and Garlic Roasted Chicken

Conversion Tables

WEIGHT EQUIVALENTS

US STANDARD	METRIC (APPROXIMATE)
1 Ounce	28 g
2 Ounces	57 g
5 Ounces	142 g
10 Ounces	284 g
15 Ounces	425 g
16 Ounces (1 Pound)	455 g
1.5 Pounds	680 g
2 Pounds	907 g

VOLUME EQUIVALENTS (DRY)

US STANDARD	METRIC (APPROXIMATE)
1/8 Teaspoon	0.5 ml
1/4 Teaspoon	1 ml
1/2 Teaspoon	2 ml
3/4 Teaspoon	4 ml
1 Teaspoon	5 ml
1 Tablespoon	15 ml
1/4 Cup	59 ml
1/2 Cup	118 ml
3/4 Cup	177 ml
1 Cup	235 ml
2 Cups	475 ml
3 Cups	700 ml
4 Cups	1 l

VOLUME EQUIVALENTS (LIQUID)

US STANDARD	US STANDARD (OUNCES)	METRIC (APPROXIMATE)
2 Tablespoons	1 fl.oz.	30 ml
1/4 Cup	2 fl.oz.	60 ml
1/2 Cup	4 fl.oz.	120 ml
1 Cup	8 fl.oz.	240 ml
1 1/2 Cups	12 fl.oz.	355 ml
2 Cups or 1 Pint	16 fl.oz.	475 ml
4 Cups or 1 Quart	32 fl.oz.	1 l
1 Gallon	128 fl.oz.	4 l

TEMPERATURES EQUIVALENTS

FAHRENHEIT (F)	CELSIUS (C) (APPROXIMATE)
225 °F	107 °C
250 °F	120 °C
275 °F	135 °C
300 °F	150 °C
325 °F	160 °C
350 °F	180 °C
375 °F	190 °C
400 °F	205 °C
425 °F	220 °C
450 °F	235 °C
475 °F	245 °C
500 °F	260 °C

Bonus

YOUR THOUGHTS MATTER!

Dear Valued Reader,

Expressing gratitude for joining us on this flavorful adventure. We trust the recipes have brought simplicity and flavor-packed wonders to your cooking experience.

YOUR FEEDBACK COUNTS

If this cookbook has infused culinary joy into your life, we invite you to share your insights by leaving a review on Amazon. Your reflections can guide prospective readers, serving as a compass for those seeking a delightful culinary journey.

Your support is truly invaluable!

HOW TO SHARE YOUR THOUGHTS:

- Visit the book's Amazon page.
- Navigate to the "Customer Reviews" section.
- Select "Write a Customer Review."
- Remember, your words carry weight!

YOUR BONUS AWAITS!

As a token of our appreciation, we're thrilled to offer you an exclusive bonus. Simply use your smartphone to scan the QR code below, and a special bonus will be delivered directly to your email.

HOW TO REDEEM YOUR BONUS:

- Activate your smartphone camera.
- Align it with the QR code.
- Once scanned, follow the on-screen instructions to claim your bonus.

Thank you again for purchasing my cookbook!
May these recipes continue to bring joy and flavor to your culinary endeavors.

Happy Cooking!

Warm Regards,
Olivia Davis

© Copyright 2024-2025 by Olivia Davis - All rights reserved.

This document is geared towards providing exact and reliable information in regards to the topic and issue covered. The publication is sold with the idea that the publisher is not required to render accounting, officially permitted, or otherwise, qualified services. If advice is necessary, legal or professional, a practiced individual in the profession should be ordered.

From a Declaration of Principles which was accepted and approved equally by a Committee of the American Bar Association and a Committee of Publishers and Associations.

In no way is it legal to reproduce, duplicate, or transmit any part of this document in either electronic means or in printed format. Recording of this publication is strictly prohibited and any storage of this document is not allowed unless with written permission from the publisher. All rights reserved.

The information provided herein is stated to be truthful and consistent, in that any liability, in terms of inattention or otherwise, by any usage or abuse of any policies, processes, or directions contained within is the solitary and utter responsibility of the recipient reader. Under no circumstances will any legal responsibility or blame be held against the publisher for any reparation, damages, or monetary loss due to the information herein, either directly or indirectly.

Respective authors and publisher own all copyrights.

The information herein is offered for informational purposes solely, and is universal as so.
The presentation of the information is without contract or any type of guarantee assurance.

The trademarks that are used are without any consent, and the publication of the trademark is without permission or backing by the trademark owner. All trademarks and brands within this book are for clarifying purposes only and are the owned by the owners themselves, not affiliated with this document.

Made in the USA
Las Vegas, NV
28 May 2024